COINAGE IN SCOTLAND

COINAGE IN SCOTLAND

J.D. Bateson

SPINK
LONDON
1997

© J.D. Bateson 1997

First published 1997

All rights reserved. No part of this publication may be
reproduced, in any form or by any means, without
permission from the Publisher

Typeset by Bernard Cavender Design & Greenwood Graphics Publishing
Printed in Great Britain by Cromwell Press Ltd, Melksham

Published by Spink & Son Ltd.
5, 6, 7 King Street, St. James's, London SW1Y 6QS

A CIP catalogue record for this book is available from
the British Library

ISBN 0 907605 74 5

Contents

	INTRODUCTION	7
	A NOTE ON TERMINOLOGY	9
	LIST OF FIGURES	10
1	ROMAN COINS FROM SCOTLAND	11
2	THE VIKINGS	27
3	A COINAGE FOR SCOTLAND	39
4	THE SILVER GROAT 1350-1550	54
5	GOLD IN MEDIEVAL SCOTLAND	74
6	BILLON AND COPPER	86
7	MARY QUEEN OF SCOTS	97
8	JAMES VI AND I	112
9	CHARLES I AND THE CIVIL WAR	129
10	RESTORATION TO UNION 1660-1707	143
	SELECT BIBLIOGRAPHY	159
	LIST OF ILLUSTRATIONS	162
	INDEX	169

Acknowledgements

I am grateful to Mr. N. L. McQ. Holmes for looking at the text and making many helpful suggestions; also for letting me see his Cramond coin report in advance of publication. Dr. Lawrence Keppie kindly read through the Roman chapter. My thanks are due to Mr. Roderick Macpherson of Glasgow for lending me a number of his Scottish coins for use in the plates (illustration numbers 40, 61-2, 82, 88, 110-11, 117, 119, 138-9, 145, 166-7, 169, 173, 183 and 193); to Dr. W. S. Hanson for letting me include coins from his excavations at Elginhaugh (4-6 and 8-10); to Professor C. D. Morris for the use of the penny from his excavations at Brough of Birsay (39); and to Mr. P. O'Hara for letting me record a small hoard of James III copper (incl.113-4) - now in the National Museums of Scotland. The remaining coins illustrated are in the Hunterian Museum and are included with the permission of the University of Glasgow; the two pieces from Leckie (21-2) are on permanent loan from Lord Younger of Leckie; and the four pennies from the Iona hoard belong to the Iona Trustees (31-4). The photographs are the work of Trevor Graham of the Glasgow University Media Services Photographic Unit and I also thank Graeme Campbell of the Hunterian Museum's Design Studio for his assistance with the maps.

Introduction

Consideration of coinage in Scotland is usually confined to the medieval period when, from the twelfth century, Scotland issued its own coins. During this time these were frequently supplemented by the use of English and other European issues. However, in two earlier periods coins appeared in some numbers. Roman coins were brought in by the army in the first, second and early third centuries AD and even after Scotland had been finally abandoned by Rome some coins trickled northwards until the beginning of the fifth century. Later Norse invaders and settlers also owned coins, mainly Anglo-Saxon silver pennies, which were deposited from late in the ninth century until the mid-eleventh century. In neither of these two periods were any coins made in Scotland nor did the imported pieces circulate in a normal manner.

The systematic recording of Roman coins found in Scotland was started by Sir George Macdonald early in the the twentieth century and continued by Professor Anne Robertson. The results were published regularly in the *Proceedings of the Society of Antiquaries of Scotland* and Professor Robertson's final record presents a detailed survey of coin use in north Britain during the Roman period (Robertson 1983). The record continues and has been published up to 1987 (Bateson 1989). Viking period hoards have been listed and discussed in two sylloges dealing respectively with the Anglo-Saxon coins in the former National Museum of Antiquities of Scotland (Stevenson 1966) and the Hiberno-Norse coins in the British Museum (Dolley 1966). The small number of single finds of this period has recently received some attention (Stevenson 1986).

David I introduced a Scottish coinage in 1136 and throughout the twelfth century there was a steady increase in coin use. A separate Scottish coinage lasted until just after the Union with England in 1707. Although there are earlier works on Scottish coins, the *magnum opus* on the series is that published in 1887 by Edward Burns entitled, *The Coinage of Scotland*. It is so extensive and thorough that it is still the standard reference for most Scottish coins and the starting point for much research. This is complemented by an exhaustive survey of the archival evidence by R. W. Cochran-Patrick in his *Records of the Coinage of Scotland* published in 1876. Records relating to the early

INTRODUCTION

issues are rather scarce but they increase after 1350. Little new material has come to light since Cochran-Patrick's work. Well over fifty years were to elapse before new interest and work on the Scottish coinage appeared. This began with Ian Stewart's *The Scottish Coinage* in 1956 and the revised edition of this, though unfortunately now out of print, remains the best introduction to the series (Stewart 1967). Among Lord Stewartby's many other articles dealing with Scottish coins may be noted the very important work on the Scottish mints (Stewart 1971) and his survey of the literature (Stewart 1981). At the same time Colonel and Mrs Murray contributed greatly to the field, particulary on the Marian issues and those of the seventeenth century. At the National Museum of Antiquities of Scotland, Robert Stevenson worked on the issues and finds of the seventeenth century and more recently on the billon of the sixteenth century.

The Oxford Symposium on Coinage in Medieval Scotland held in 1977 provided a timely opportunity to review the situation and address some of the outstanding questions and uncertainties. The Proceedings provides a valuable record of this and includes an updated and expanded listing of Scottish coin hoards deposited up to 1600 as well as some discussion of other coin finds (Metcalf 1977). The recording of coin finds from Scotland was subsequently expanded to include medieval finds, and those made during the following decade up to 1987 have now also been published (Bateson 1989).

The Seaby series of popular catalogues of British coins contains a very useful and well illustrated guide to Scottish coins (Seaby and Purvey 1982) while a basic introduction is available in the Shire series (Bateson 1987). Booklets have also appeared on the Edinburgh (Holmes 1982) and St Andrews mints (Smart 1991). One sylloge has been published on Scottish coins, that combining the important collections of the Ashmolean Museum, Oxford, and the Hunterian Museum, Glasgow (Bateson and Mayhew 1987).

Apart from these, many articles and notes on the subject have appeared in the Proceedings of the Society of Antiquaries of Scotland, the British Numismatic Journal, the Numismatic Chronicle and Spink's Numismatic Circular. A great debt is owed to all this literature in bringing together both the issues and their circulation in the present work.

A note on terminology

A note on coin names and the systems may be of use to those unfamiliar with numismatic terms:

Roman
The Roman Imperial system in use until the mid-third century AD consisted of

gold aureus = 25 denarii
silver denarius = 4 sestertii
brass sestertius = 4 asses
brass dupondius = 2 asses
copper as = 4 quadrantes
copper quadrans

Anglo-Saxon
The early Anglo-Saxon silver penny of the seventh and eighth centuries is known as the sceat (plur. sceattas). The sceat was replaced by a larger and thinner silver penny during the reign of Offa (757-96) and this remained the main coin struck in Britain for over 500 years. However, the Kingdom of Northumbria continued to strike sceattas, which became debased early in the ninth century and are usually known as stycas.

Medieval
The medieval Scots pound (like the pound sterling) consisted of 240 pennies (240d) as opposed to the modern decimal pound of 100 pennies (100p).

pound = 240d
shilling = 12d

Although Scotland struck some merk pieces, the merk (English mark) was generally used as a unit of account, equal to thirteen shillings and four pence (13s 4d) and this was used later as a coin denomination.

The groat was a larger coin related to the penny; in Scotland this initially had the value of 4d, as in England, but many other values occurred later. Thus the early parity between the Scottish and English coinages (1d Scots = 1d English or sterling) was broken in the latter half of the fourteenth century and the two coinages differed at an increasing rate until the Act of Union: (see figure 4.1)

List of Figures

1.1 Roman Scotland: sites noted in the text	12
2.1 Finds of Northumbrian stycas; silver hoards and stray pennies	28
2.2 Finds of Viking-age silver from Orkney	31
3.1 Alexander III's long cross mints	44
4.1 Comparison of Scottish and English groats	72

CHAPTER ONE
Roman coins from Scotland

Coins first came to Scotland with the Roman cohorts. The Roman army advanced northwards on three occasions: in the late first century AD under the Governor of Britain, Agricola; in the early 140s when the Antonine Wall was constructed as the northern frontier of the province; and in the first decade of the third century in the great imperial expedition led by the Emperor, Septimius Severus. For the most part Roman activity was confined to the Lowlands, with some extension up the east coast.

The native population encountered by the Romans neither produced nor used coins and indeed there is no certain evidence that any coin reached Scotland before Agricola's invasion in 79.

Each of the Roman occupations of Scotland was short-lived. The country was, therefore, never more than a frontier area. Camps, forts and roads were constructed but no more. There was never enough time for Romanization, and Scotland possesses no Roman towns, no villas and no temples. Coinage was thus confined to the military. It was brought north for the pay of the soldiers, for provisions and perhaps for political purposes in the form of subsidies or bribes. These same soldiers would also have brought their own money with them: their savings – their hoards – and small change.

In the forts the soldiers received their pay but suffered a string of deductions for such items as food, arms and burial club subscription. How much coin was actually transferred to them is not certain. At the time of Agricola's invasion the legionary's basic pay was 225 denarii per year though in 84 Domitian increased this to 300 denarii. Officers received much more and auxiliary troops rather less but overall the army in Scotland required large sums of money, though it is only a very small proportion of this which has survived as coin finds and in coin hoards. These represent coins accidentally lost and hoards which for some reason were not recovered by their owners.

Coins were lost in and around the forts, especially in the barrack blocks and the bath-house. For example, at least fifteen denarii and six bronzes were recovered during the excavation of the barrack blocks at Newstead and many of the coins found at Elginhaugh also came from

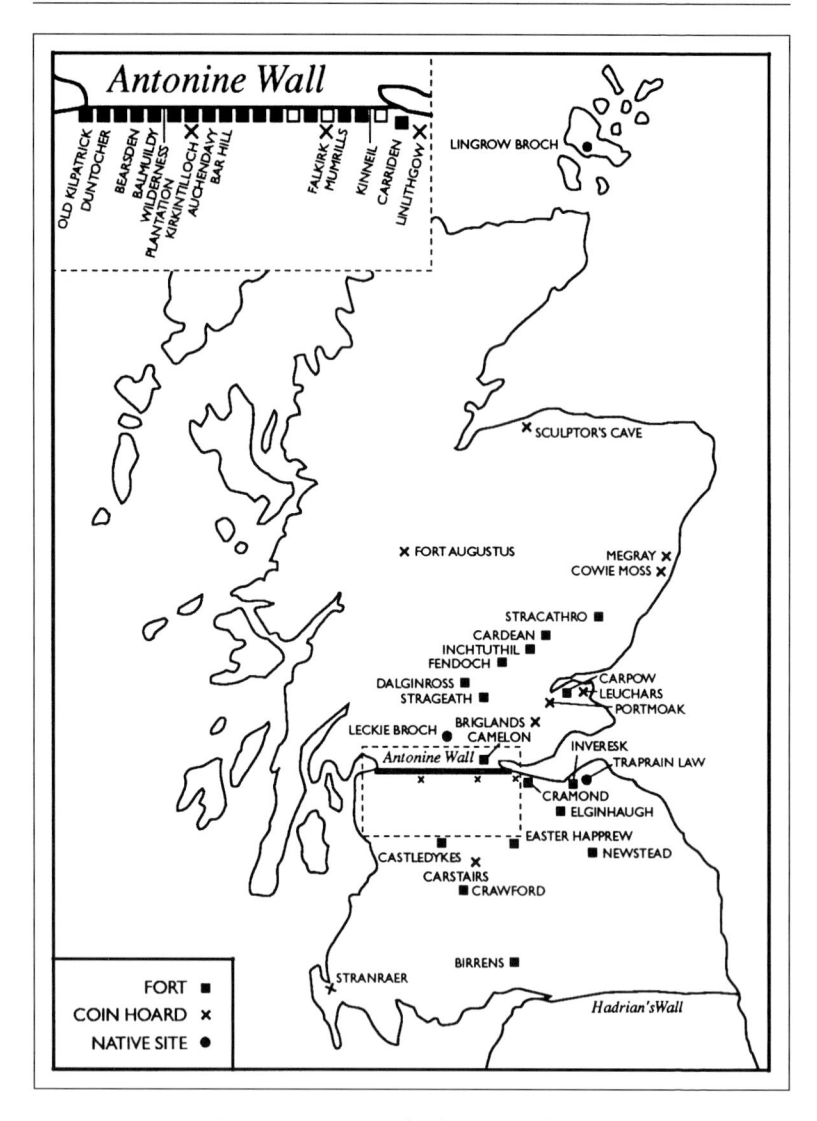

Fig. 1.1 Roman Scotland: sites noted in text.

the barrack blocks. One was found in the changing-room of the bath-house at Bearsden (1) and another, an as of Antoninus Pius, was found wedged between two of the flag-stones of the floor in one of the warm-rooms. No fewer than nine denarii and thirteen bronzes were recovered in the baths at Newstead.

1 Antoninus Pius for Marcus Aurelius, dupondius or as, AD 153-4, found in the changing-room of the bath-house at Bearsden.

Equally there needed to be a safe deposit for the fort's funds. The pay-chest was usually kept with the standards in the central office at the the rear of the headquarters building. This room, the aedes, often possessed a sunken 'treasury' pit or cellar. Two denarii were found on the floor of the aedes at Crawford and another was likewise discovered at Balmuildy. Excavation of the pit in the aedes at Old Kilpatrick produced a denarius of Vespasian (*2*) and another of Faustina I. Periods of exertion such as construction and demolition probably occasioned opportunities for coins to be lost by members of the work-party. Five of the six coins from Cardean were found in construction levels and many have been recovered in destruction contexts such as the one from demolition debris at Crawford.

2 Vespasian, denarius, AD 69-70, found in the aedes at Old Kilpatrick.

It was usual for civil settlements to spring up beside the forts to supply the extra needs of the troops and these also allowed small-scale trading to develop. Little, however, is known of the vici in Scotland, for

3 Trajan, denarius, AD 103-11, found in the annexe at Balmuildy.

investigation has tended to concentrate on the forts themselves. Most forts possess one or more annexes but an annexe does not necessarily mean a civilian settlement (3). The existence of one vicus is shown by reference to its inhabitants on an altar dedicated to Jupiter found at Carriden but the most extensive investigation of a supposed vicus has been that carried out at Inveresk, Midlothian, to the east of the Antonine fort there. The large number of coins recovered recently at Castledykes all appear to have been found outside the fort, again perhaps pointing to the existance of a substantial civilian settlement. It is clear that civilian settlements did exist and it is in these that Roman Scotland may have approached coin use in the normal sense.

It was probably through such settlements that some Roman coins 'drifted' into native hands and found their way to native sites. Also payment for supplies and gifts to friendly tribes or bribes to hostile ones may have resulted in quite large sums reaching native possession, and undoubtedly occasional theft or looting increased this. The coin finds and hoards dating from after the Severan abandonment of Scotland present more of a problem, but raiding, trade and mercenary activity may account for most.

The total number of Roman coins recorded as having been found on Roman forts, native sites and in unassociated contexts in Scotland now exceeds 1,750. To this may be added a figure of perhaps about 7,000 coins contained in over 40 hoards. Thus somewhat fewer than 10,000 coins have been recovered dating from the first to fourth centuries, though the country received very few of the later base coins found in huge numbers further south. Nevertheless the corpus of Roman coin finds from Scotland is not large, especially if set against those recovered from some of the larger sites in England. However, careful study of the Scottish finds has yielded much information about coin use there at that time, despite the sparse recording of finds until this century and the generally poor condition of many of the coins.

The fort at Newstead, near Melrose in Roxburghshire, is one of the largest and most important of Roman military sites in Scotland and also the most prolific in terms of coin finds. Since the late eighteenth century it has yielded a coin series which now numbers in excess of 400 pieces. These date from the Republic to Crispina, the wife of Commodus, and include gold, silver and bronze coins. That issued for Crispina would appear to date the final abandonment of Newstead to the 180s though a small number of third and fourth century bronze coins suggest the occasional visitor. The fort was founded by Agricola in 79 or 80 and demolished about 87 but it was soon re-built to be occupied until the end of the century or even beyond, if the little hoard of four denarii, including two only slightly worn pieces of Trajan of 103-11, belongs to this period. Again there were two periods of occupation in the Antonine period, the second running from about 158. As with many sites occupied in both Flavian and Antonine times, it is not always easy to distinguish which period saw the loss of first-century issues since these, particularly in gold and silver, often circulated into the second century.

Consequently those sites occupied only in either the Flavian or Antonine period are of especial interest. The most important of these is Inchtuthil, the legionary fortress on the Tay, demolished before it was even completed about 87. Excavations have recovered eight coins, asses only: one of Vespasian and seven of Domitian, among which those of certain date all belong to 86. North-east of Inchtuthil lie the Flavian forts of Cardean and Stracathro. Two denarii and four bronzes of Vespasian were recovered from the former and a single as of 86 from the latter. Southwards, in Perthshire, the fort at Fendoch has produced a denarius of Galba while from Dalginross has come a gold aureus of Titus and yet another as of 86.

Other Flavian forts have produced no coins at all, but a large group was recovered during the extensive excavations at Elginhaugh in 1986 and 1987. Fifty-four coins were recovered, six denarii (**4-6**) and the rest mainly Flavian or earlier bronzes of which the latest is of 86. In addition, a hoard of forty-five denarii, possibly a ritual foundation deposit, was found buried in the principia. As with the other denarii, the hoard is mostly composed of Republican issues over a century old though the latest piece is a slightly worn issue of Domitian issued by Vespasian in 77-8. This is one of the larger groups of coin finds from a Roman site in Scotland and seems to date the occupation of this single period site from 79 or 80 to 87.

4 *Julius Caesar, denarius, 49-48 BC, found at Elginhaugh.*

5 *Brutus and Cassius, denarius, 43-42 BC, found at Elginhaugh.*

6 *Plated hybrid denarius of Vespasian and Vitellius, AD 73, found at Elginhaugh.*

The small hoard of aureii from Broomholm, Dumfriesshire, suggests some gold reached Scotland and among the finds of single first-century gold coins there may well be Flavian losses, especially some of those of Nero, now recorded from ten sites including two from Newstead. However, silver was the more usual coin used by the army. Coin hoards from Britain show that Republican denarii had more or less disappeared by the reign of Hadrian though still accounting for up to forty per cent of the currency until the end of the first century. Only the legionary denarii of Mark Antony continued in use, even into the third century (7). Republican coins, excepting the latter, and probably also pre-Neronian imperial coins found in Scotland, therefore appear to represent Flavian losses. Denarii seem to have been present in some numbers during that period as shown by the number recovered at Elginhaugh.

However, a large proportion of the coins brought by the Flavian army appears to have been bronze, particularly the as. Most of these,

7 Mark Antony, legionary denarius (Leg. V), 32-31 BC, found at Bearsden.

8 Vespasian, Fides as, struck at Lyons (with globe at end of neck), AD 77-8, found outside the officers' quarters end of barrack block 5 at Elginhaugh.

like those found in the rest of Britain, belong to quite specific issues from the mint of Lyons, indicated by the use of a small globe placed at the end of the emperor's neck. Two groups are involved, minted in 70-73 and 77-8 and including reverses depicting Fides (**8**), Fortuna and an eagle on a globe. Such pieces have been found at the Flavian sites of Elginhaugh, Cardean and Easter Happrew and at the Flavian/Antonine sites at Newstead, Strageath and Crawford. Another group, of Domitian and struck only at Rome, consists of bronzes of 84, 85 and especially 86 among which an as depicting Moneta is frequent. These are usually in virtually unworn condition indicating loss soon after their arrival (**9-10**). There is no certain bronze coin later than this from a Flavian site in Scotland, except Newstead, and though few such coins were struck by Domitian after 86, it is the lack of wear and hence circulation which indicates that the Roman occupation of north Britain came to an end about 87. Such pieces have been found on at

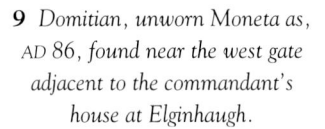

9 Domitian, unworn Moneta as, AD 86, found near the west gate adjacent to the commandant's house at Elginhaugh.

10 Domitian, unworn Moneta as, AD 85, found in the destruction level of the officers' quarters of barrack block 5 at Elginhaugh.

least ten forts and in some instances are associated with the demolition of the fort. Coins of this group have not been found on the forts of the Antonine Wall thus confirming their Flavian use and loss.

Although some Flavian sites were re-occupied in the Antonine period, new forts appeared which thus too are of a single period. The main group of these constitutes a major element in one of the greatest monuments of the Roman frontier world, the Antonine Wall. In the early 140s the Governor of Roman Britain, Lollius Urbicus, seems to have engaged the tribes north of Hadrian's Wall. A sestertius was struck in 143-4 giving Antoninus Pius his new imperial acclamation, IMPERATOR II, and depicting Victory on the reverse with the word BRITAN across the field (**11**). The victory implied was followed by the building of the new wall across central Scotland from the Forth to the Clyde.

11 Antoninus Pius, sestertius, AD 143, with Victory and BRITAN on reverse.

There were two phases of occupation, for about the mid-150s the Antonine Wall was briefly abandoned. There appears to have been unrest in northern Britain about this time and associated with its suppression are asses of 154-5 showing a dejected figure of Britannia on the reverse (12). Two such coins were found at the fort of Birrens in Annandale. The final abandonment of the Antonine Wall may have taken place in the 160s but the coin evidence for this is disappointing.

12 Antoninus Pius, as, AD 154-5, with Britannia on the reverse.

The total number of recorded coin finds from the Antonine Wall now exceeds 170. Between Carriden in the east and Old Kilpatrick in the west there were at least seventeen forts and perhaps as many as forty fortlets. Fifteen of the forts have yielded one or more coins. Mumrills with thirty-nine pieces possesses the largest group which is made up of twelve denarii and twenty-seven bronzes, of which eleven are sestertii. Bar Hill too has a relatively large corpus of thirteen denarii and twelve bronzes in addition to an unusual group recovered from the well. Situated in the principia, this yielded two official silver denarii, ten tin copies and the copper core of a plated copy, all possibly thrown into the well as offerings unless the copies represent hastily discarded forgeries (13-16). Excavations at Balmuildy, Bearsden and Old Kilpatrick have unearthed sixteen, thirteen and nineteen coins respectively. Among the fortlets Kinneil and Wilderness Plantation have each produced a single coin.

The finds from the Wall give an indication of the coinage during the Antonine period in Scotland. Gold has been found on three Antonine Wall sites: one of Vespasian at Carriden, another of Trajan at Auchendavy, and two, of Vespasian and Hadrian, at Duntocher. An aureus of Vespasian was lost in an Antonine I context, i.e. before 158, at the fort of Birrens in the south-west and five have been recovered at Newstead. A few have been found on native sites but nearly half of the

13 Tin copy of denarius of Trajan, AD 112-17, from the well at Bar Hill.

14 Tin copy of denarius of Trajan, AD 112-17, from the well at Bar Hill.

15 Tin copy of denarius of Trajan, AD 112-17, from the well at Bar Hill.

16 Tin copy of denarius of Trajan, AD 112-17, from the well at Bar Hill.

total of about forty pieces are isolated finds. Two thirds are first century issues. It would seem therefore that gold was reasonably common in this period and that some of it found its way into native hands presumably via trade.

However, silver denarii constitute the main type of coin found on sites and almost without exception in the hoards. Virtually every fort on the Antonine Wall has produced silver, especially Mumrills, Old Kilpatrick and Bearsden where in each case a third of the coins recovered are denarii. Over 130 denarii have come from Newstead, around half of which are second century issues. Nine out of the ten hoards ending with coins of Antoninus Pius and his family are of denarii, ranging in size up to the 300 or so found in a jar at Linlithgow. However, the Antonine issues are outnumbered by those of Hadrian and Trajan but this is the expected pattern, for it is now recognized that the coins of any emperor will not predominate immediately in the coinage in circulation and may not do so until some time after his death. This pattern is repeated in the hoards.

Bronze coins are still common. The only hoard of such from the first and second centuries appears to have consisted of over 100 sestertii, up to Marcus Aurelius as Caesar, found at Carstairs, Lanarkshire. At Antonine Newstead losses of bronze coins are about the same in number as those of denarii. Among fifty published sestertii, thirty-eight are of the second century by which time they are more common than the dupondii and asses together. Although silver seems more numerous in the Antonine levels at Birrens, among the bronze sestertii again predominate. The sestertius is also the most common denomination of the second-century issues from Strageath.

The coins which greatly interest historians and archaeologists are the latest datable pieces from the Antonine Wall. These might be expected to answer the much debated question of when the Wall was abandoned, but unfortunately the numismatic evidence simply lacks the numbers of relevant pieces to be conclusive. The latest stratified coin, recovered from the granary of the fort at Old Kilpatrick, is a fairly worn denarius issued by Antoninus Pius between 164 and 169 for his daughter Lucilla, wife of Marcus Aurelius (17). From the fort annexe at Mumrills comes the stray find of an as of Marcus Aurelius of 174, again in fairly worn condition. The former would thus suggest occupation down to at least 165 while the latter points to at least 175. The reports of two coins of Commodus from Kirkintilloch and Bar Hill are too vague and uncertain respectively to use as further evidence on the matter. Currently the consensus, based mainly on the pottery evidence, appears to accept a date in the 160s.

17 The latest certain coin find from a site on the Antonine Wall: Marcus Aurelius for Lucilla, denarius, AD 164-9, found at Old Kilpatrick.

Just to the north of the Wall, west of Falkirk, lies the large and strategically important fort of Camelon. Often associated with the Antonine Wall, it is nevertheless a multi-period site having its foundation in the Flavian period. It has yielded almost as many coins as the total from the Antonine Wall. Among the 140 coins found is a gold aureus struck by Trajan for his wife Plotina. The majority of the forty-one denarii are likely to be Antonine losses though the worn Republican denarii and the single specimens of Augustus and Otho probably belong to the Flavian occupation. The as with twenty-three first-century examples seems to have been the main coin at that time while the second-century coins of this denomination number thirteen. The eighteen second-century sestertii outnumber the five of the first century. The latest coin from the Antonine levels here is an as struck by Marcus Aurelius possibly in 174.

Other such groups have come from the multi-period forts at Birrens, Strageath and Castledykes. Birrens, in Dumfriesshire, the most southerly of Scotland's Roman forts, has yielded fifty-two coins including a fairly worn aureus of Vespasian of 70 from an Antonine context. Included are seven worn legionary denarii of Mark Antony and a further seventeen imperial denarii. There are forty-two coins from Strageath, Perthshire, starting with one Republican and four legionary denarii and ending with a single issue of Antoninus Pius. The latter proved to be the copper core of a plated denarius and also of note is a little quadrans of Domitian, probably from the demolition level of the Flavian fort. Most of the sixty coins from Castledykes, Lanarkshire, are recent unstratified finds from the area to the south of the fort. Dates of issue range from the Republic to the 140s.

18 *Commodus, sestertius,* AD *184-5, with title* BRIT *at end of obverse legend and* VICT BRIT *in exergue on reverse.*

CHAPTER TWO

The Vikings

It was almost five hundred years before coins appeared again in Scotland. Once more they were brought in by foreigners though by now Vikings who came from Norway by way of the northern isles and down the west coast. Paradoxically the coins they possessed came mostly from the south – silver pennies of the Anglo-Saxon kings along with some European deniers and more exotic dirhams from the Middle East. Most belong to the period from about 900 to 1050 and are to be associated with a pattern of settlement rather than raiding and looting. Furthermore the coins are often found with other forms of silver, such as ingots and hack-silver, and appear to have been used as bullion rather than coinage.

However, there is a small group of earlier coins belonging to the ninth century. These are stycas of the Anglo-Saxon kingdom of Northumbria which in the eighth century had stretched northwards to the Forth and in the ninth still extended to the Tweed. Such small copper coins are a debased form, from about 820, of earlier silver sceattas which in the rest of England had been replaced by a larger silver penny from the end of the eighth century. Stycas were issued in very large numbers and appear to have been extensively used throughout the Northumbrian kingdom until the fall of York to Danish Vikings in 867. A number were recovered near Abbey Bridge in Jedburgh in 1834 and later a single piece, of Aethelred II's second reign of 844-9, was found elsewhere in the town. A base silver styca of Eanbald, Archbishop of York (796-830), was discovered in the churchyard of Coldingham, Berwickshire, while others of Eanred (810-41) and Aethelred II's first reign (841-4) have been found at Aberlady and Dunbar, both in East Lothian.

In the west excavations at Whithorn Priory have recovered over fifty base silver and copper stycas while, also in Wigtownshire, the Glenluce sandhills have yielded more than a dozen Northumbrian issues (**23-26**). From the same area, at Talnotrie in Kirkcudbrightshire, comes a small hoard of jewellery, including six stycas. Another hoard, found at Paisley in Renfrewshire, seems to have consisted of a 'considerable number' of stycas only.

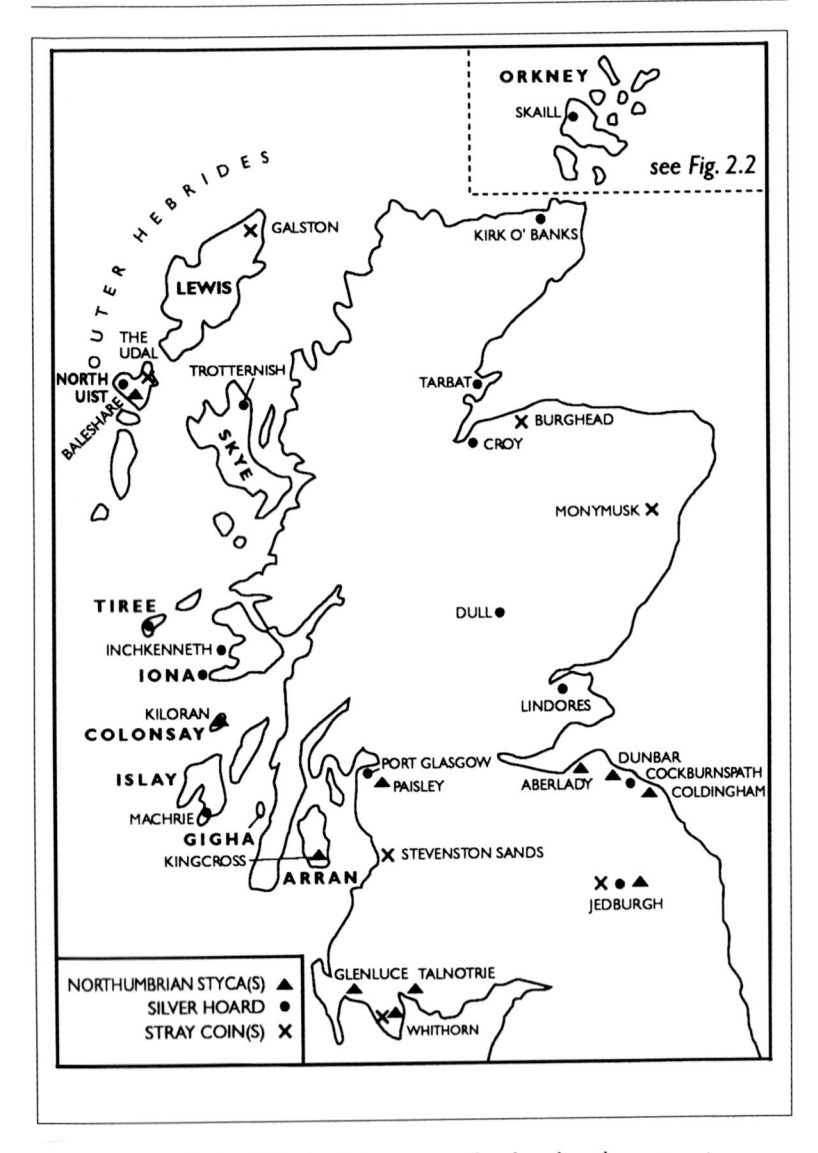

Fig. 2.1 Finds of Northumbrian stycas; silver hoards and stray pennies.

Three finds of stycas have been made on the western isles. The grave goods of a Norse burial at Kingcross Point on Arran included a single piece of Archbishop Wigmund (837-54). A Viking boat burial at Kiloran Point on Colonsay possessed three stycas of which two, both pierced, are issues of Aethelred II and Archbishop Wigmund.

23 Eanred (810-41), styca, moneyer Eadwin.

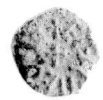

24 Eanred, styca, moneyer Fordred.

25 Aethelred II, first reign (841-4), styca, moneyer Tidwulf.

26 Aethelred II, second reign (844-9), styca, moneyer Eardwulf.

Nos. 23-6 are probably from the Glenluce Sands, Wigtownshire.

27 Aethelred II, first reign, styca, moneyer Eanred, found 1988 on the sandhills at Baleshare, North Uist. [enlarged x 2]

Another styca of Aethelred II was found by chance on sandhills at Baleshare on North Uist (**27**). These three finds probably constitute Viking souvenirs but those from the mainland may have had some currency function.

The earliest find containing Anglo-Saxon silver pennies seems to be that from Croy, Inverness-shire, hidden about 850. This small hoard, mainly of beads and some silver, included a penny of Coenwulf of Mercia (796-821) and another pierced penny of Aethelwulf of Wessex (839-58). The Talnotrie find contained besides the stycas, four pennies of Burgred of Mercia (852-74), a denier of Louis the Pious and two dirhams. The pennies date deposition to about 875. Over half a century elapses before hoards appear again when three with issues of Aethelstan (924-39) were concealed. That from Trotternish on Skye included 110 coins and 23 pieces of silver, mainly ingots; the coins were mostly of Edward the Elder and Aethelstan besides some dirhams, mainly Samanid issues of 892-942. About the same time, circa 935, a large hoard of coins of Aethelstan with a single fragment of a silver necklace was buried at Cockburnspath, Berwickshire.

Around 950 there was hidden at Skaill on Orkney the largest Viking-age silver hoard recorded from Scotland. Weighing up to eight kilograms, the bulk of the contents comprised whole and fragmentary brooches, armlets, necklaces, finger-rings, penannular armlets known as 'ring-money' and ingots. Twenty-one coins were also recovered, of which two are pennies of Aethelstan and the Vikings of York while the remainder are all fragmentary Samanid and Abbasid dirhams struck no later than 946.

The date of deposition of four hoards appears to centre on 975. The ninety coins and four ingots recovered at Machrie on Islay seem to

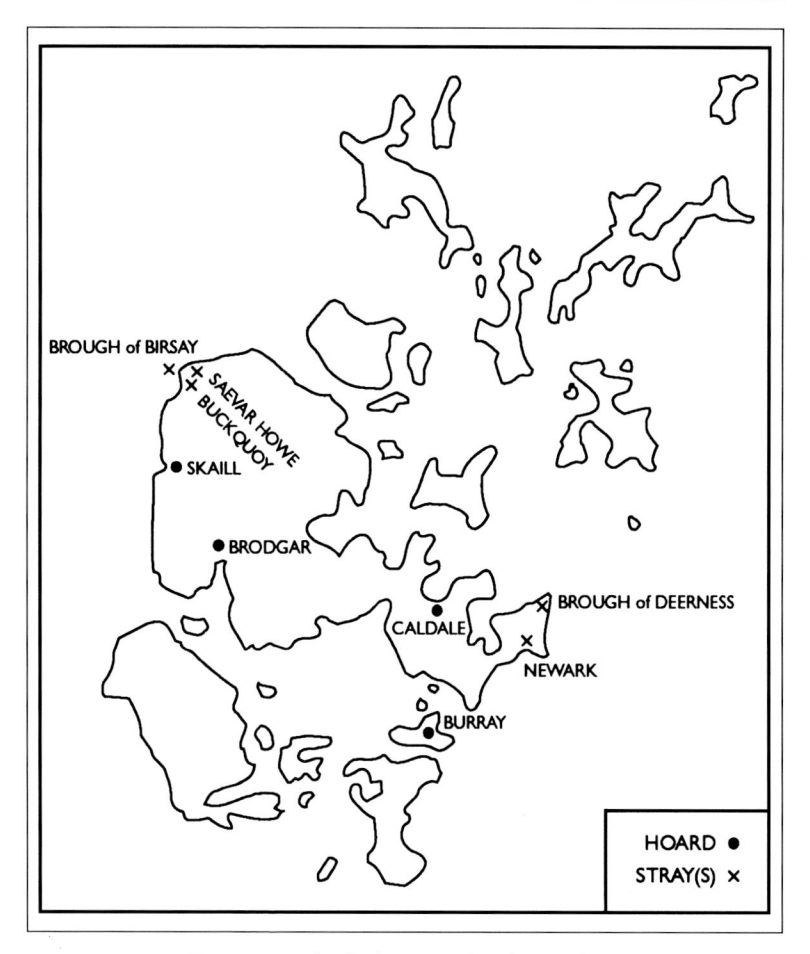

Fig. 2.2 Finds of Viking-age silver from Orkney

constitute only a small part of the hoard found there in 1850. The coins are mostly of Eadgar of issues prior to his reform of 973 (**28-30**); there was also a dirham and a denier of Cologne. A rather vague hoard of a 'great number' of coins and possibly a few pieces of silver found at Port Glasgow may have been buried at this time. Grave digging at Tarbet churchyard, Ross-shire, unearthed a small hoard of thirteen coins and four pieces of ring-money. Twelve of these coins are tenth-century Frankish deniers while the single Anglo-Saxon penny belongs to Eadgar's pre-reform issue. The fourth find of this group was made on Tiree and seems to have been composed of coins only, perhaps as many as 500 and again ending with Eadgar.

28 Machrie hoard (Islay), Eadgar (959-75), penny, moneyer Durand.

29 Machrie hoard, Eadgar, penny (fragmentary), moneyer ?Wiferth.

30 Machrie hoard, Eadgar, penny (fragmentary), uncertain moneyer.

A further four hoards belong to the final quarter of the tenth century. A considerable number of coins, of which one was of Aethelred II (978-1016), appears to have been hidden on North Uist in the decade 980-90 without any associated silver objects. The bulk of the hoard found at the Abbot's House on Iona consists of coins of Eadgar and has been likened to those hidden at the time of the Battle of Tara in 980 (**31-34**). However, this hoard of about 350 coins and a few ornaments made its way to Iona where some pennies of Aethelred II were added, including two struck between 985 and 991. Its deposition has been associated with the sack of Iona in 986.

A wooden bowl unearthed during peat-cutting at Burray, Orkney, contained around two kilograms of ring-money and hack-silver as well as a dozen coins ending with Aethelred II and suggesting concealment about 998. A hoard of about 100 coins and some silver found on Inchkenneth in the Hebrides is probably just slightly later and contains

31 Iona hoard, Eadred (946-55), penny, moneyer Thurmod.

32 Iona hoard, Eadwig (955-9), penny, moneyer Heriger.

33 Iona hoard, Eadgar (959-75), penny, moneyer Grid.

34 Iona hoard, Eadgar, penny, moneyer Fastolf.

a few early Hiberno-Norse pennies of Dublin and some continental deniers. About the same time another hoard was being concealed at Quendale on Shetland but, dispersed after finding, the exact number of coins and ring-money is unknown (35-37).

35 *Quendale hoard (Shetland), Eadwig (955-9), penny, moneyer Aescwulf.*

36 *Quendale hoard, Eadgar (959-75), penny, moneyer Heriger.*

37 *Quendale hoard, Aethelred II (978-1016), penny, crux type (991-7), York, moneyer Wulfsige.*

A single fused rouleau of at least sixteen phase II Dublin pennies found recently at Dull, Perthshire, is the only certain hoard composed solely of Hiberno-Norse issues to have been found anywhere in Scotland. It may have been hidden about 1025. A large hoard of coins, including Cnut's helmet type of 1024-30, and some gold ornaments, from Lindores, Fife, has been dated to circa 1030. The find of about 100 coins and a single piece of silver from Bongate, Jedburgh, may belong slightly earlier while that from Caldale, Kirkwall, Orkney, consisting of around 300 coins and a great amount of silver, probably all ring-money, may be somewhat later, about 1035. A single Norwegian coin of Harald Hardrada is all that survives from a find of coins and ring-money discovered at Dunrossness on Shetland. Dated to about 1065 it would seem to be the latest of the Viking-age hoards from Scotland.

Besides the hoards, there are over twenty finds of single coins recovered from fourteen sites by way of excavation or chance. Pennies of Beonna of East Anglia (circa 758), Eadgar, Cnut and the Vikings of Dublin have been recovered from Whithorn Priory. Three sites in Jedburgh have yielded pennies of Aethelstan, Eadgar and Aethelred II respectively. A single tenth-century dirham was recovered on the Stevenston Sands, Ardeer, Ayrshire, while on the Hebridean islands of Lewis and North Uist, Galston and The Udal have yielded respectively a coin of Eadgar and one of Harald Hardrada of circa 1055-65. A further eight pieces, mainly of tenth-century date, have come from various sites on Orkney while Jarlshof on Shetland has yielded another penny of Aethelred II. Finally a penny of Alfred the Great's first coinage (circa 871-5) was found on the native settlement site at Burghead, Morayshire.

The majority of Viking-age coin finds thus come from hoards, and hoards which very often also contain other silver objects whose function appears to be bullion rather than ornament. It is not surprising therefore that there also exist hoards of silver lacking any coins. These have been termed 'coinless hoards' such as that from Kirk o' Banks, Caithness, consisting of eight pieces of ring-money and another from Brodgar, Orkney, of nine pieces of ring-money. There are too a small number of stray single finds of the same nature, such as the example of ring-money from Jarlshof.

Ring-money is such a common feature of finds from Viking-age Scotland that it appears to be a form of specially manufactured 'primitive' currency rather than simply a rather plain form of personal adornment. Ring-money consists of plain, penannular rings of silver, of bracelet size and of circular or lozenge-shaped cross-section (38).

pennies from Cockburnspath and the various finds from Jedburgh, though these might be regarded as an outlier of coin use in northern England.

If it is correct to regard the two earliest hoards, from Croy and Talnotrie, as native, then the first Viking find seems to be the single penny from Saevar Howe, Orkney, and the earliest hoards belong to the second quarter of the tenth century when three deposits with coins of Aethelstan were made: those at Trotternish and Cockburnspath about 935 and that from Skaill around the middle of the century. A further group of four finds all containing coins of Eadgar have been dated circa 975 while another six, with coins of Aethelred II, run up to the end of the millennium. Later, coins of Cnut have turned up in the Lindores, Jedburgh (Bongate) and Caldale finds while just slightly earlier is the Dull find. Thereafter there is only the tenuous Dunrossness hoard possibly to be consigned to the 1060s.

The majority of the coins are Anglo-Saxon pennies. A few belong to the ninth century but most are tenth-century issues, of Aethelstan, Eadgar, and Aethelred II along with some of Cnut from the next century including those of his last issue struck from 1030 to 1035/6. Arab dirhams were found in the Talnotrie, Trotternish and Skaill hoards as well as a single such piece on the sands at Stevenston, Ayrshire, but none seems to have been deposited after 950. On the other hand, apart from the denier of Louis the Pious in the Talnotrie find, the continental deniers all occur in hoards hidden after 950. These range from issues of Cologne in the Machrie and Inchkenneth hoards to more common finds of Frankish pieces, especially of Normandy. However, none seems to have been deposited after 1000, unless it is correct that some were indeed included in the Lindores find. Note might be made of the gold dinar, minted at Marrakesh in 1097, found in the churchyard at Monymusk, Aberdeenshire, but this piece may have been lost later and would therefore be a medieval rather than a Viking-age find.

There are few instances of the Hiberno-Norse issues, which commenced about 997, from Scotland. Some early Dublin pennies were included in the Inchkenneth find and the small Dull hoard seems to have consisted of early phase II pennies only, thus suggesting a date of deposit circa 1025. A single phase III penny was excavated at Whithorn and could have been lost as late as 1050. Only three coins from Norway itself have been found. Two of Harald Hardrada were probably lost in the 1060s at The Udal on North Uist and at Dunrossness on Shetland. Another of Olav Kyrre of circa 1080, from the graveyard at the Brough of Birsay, is the latest coin find from this period.

CHAPTER THREE
A Coinage for Scotland

A native coinage came about as a result of another invasion though on this occasion of England by the Scots. In 1136 David I moved south in support of his niece, the Empress Matilda, in her fight for the English throne. This had been snatched by Stephen on the death of Matilda's father, Henry I, at the end of the previous year. David quickly captured Carlisle where a mint had been set up late in Henry's reign to coin locally mined silver. The Carlisle mint became the nucleus of Scotland's own coinage and the earliest coins may have been those of Henry I's last type, in David's name.

It has been said that the issue of coins was the next stage in the use of coinage which was already well-known in Scotland in the early twelfth century. This is based on the inclusion of money sums in royal grants to various religious foundations throughout Scotland and often situated within the burghs. However, there is no known find of an English penny of this period from Scotland despite the large number struck subsequent to the Norman conquest of 1066 and no hoards since those of the late Viking period over fifty years earlier. The documentary evidence cannot be ignored but the extent of coin use in Scotland prior to 1136 is still unclear.

Pennies similar to the contemporary English ones and even bearing the name of Stephen were struck at Carlisle. However, since less than two months had elapsed between the latter's seizure of the throne and the Scottish capture of Carlisle, it is most unlikely that these pennies were struck so quickly and they must represent products of the mint when under David's control. They are in reality Scottish coins, and when further similar pieces were struck with David's name and the mint name of Edinburgh, as well as Carlisle, a Scottish coinage was well under way. Erebald was the moneyer or mint official responsible for their striking at Edinburgh and he was also one of the Carlisle moneyers.

Stephen-type pennies seem to have been struck up to around 1140 when others of cruder style and often illegible inscription appeared. During these two periods coins in the name of David's heir, Prince Henry, were struck at Carlisle, Corbridge and Bamburgh – probably in his role as an English baron for he was also Earl of Huntingdon and Northumberland. Issues other then those of the king were not usual in Britain, but are symptomatic of the unsettled conditions of Stephen's reign when local and baronial coins were often struck.

40 *David I, period C, penny, Roxburgh, Hugo, about 1150.*

Sometime during the 1140s David introduced his main coinage with a large cross fleury and pellets on the reverse. The obverse depicts a royal bust with sceptre and the inscription DAVID REX while the name of the moneyer and mint are given on the reverse. The issue was now much larger and mints operated at Carlisle, Roxburgh, Berwick, St Andrews, Perth and Aberdeen. The coins of Hugo at Roxburgh are most common (**40**) but more is known of the moneyer at St Andrews called Meinard. He appears to be the same person who is recorded as being the bishop's factor. His property probably lay at the west end of South Street but there is no evidence that his workshop was there and security would suggest a more likely siting of the mint in the castle.

It is uncertain how long these cross fleury pennies were struck but David died in 1153, a year after the death of Prince Henry, and it may have been about this time that they were replaced by poorer quality pieces of the same type but with blundered or meaningless legends. Such pieces seem to have been struck in the early years of Malcolm IV's reign and perhaps for a considerable period after though some cross fleury pennies, struck at Roxburgh and perhaps Berwick, bear the legend MALCOLM REX. Again cross fleury pennies with the name WILELMVS appeared after the accession of William the Lion in 1165 and continued for at least the first five years of his reign.

Finds of the early Scottish coins struck between 1136 and 1170 are scarce and indicate that coin use was still relatively restricted. Hoards are known from Bute and an 'unknown location' on the mainland while single finds of David coins have been made at St Nicholas' Church, Aberdeen, at St Andrews and Lochmaben and one of Prince Henry has been found at Jedburgh.

About 1170 William I instituted the 'crescent and pellet' coinage named after the type found on the reverse. This was issued over a long period and the main division is based on the shape of the sceptre head in front of the King's bust. This takes the form of either a cross potent or a cross pommée similar to those found on English pence before and after 1180. This date, however, provides only a *terminus post quem* for the Scottish change and ordering is further complicated by the conditions of the Treaty of Falaise of 1174 whereby William, having opted for the losing French side against Henry II of England, was forced to do homage for his realm and hand over the castles of Edinburgh, Berwick and Roxburgh. These were presumably not available for mints until recovered, Edinburgh in 1186 and the other two in 1189.

41 *William I, crescent and pellet penny, with pommée sceptre head, Edinburgh, Adam, 1186-95.*

The earlier group of William's crescent and pellet coinage with the potent sceptre head occurs with moneyers' names only as well as with the name of Roxburgh and more interestingly Perth. Perth seems to have been the major source of coins during the period of the loss of the castles but when exactly it was replaced and when the change in sceptre head was made are both uncertain. The later group with the pommée sceptre head is known mostly from Roxburgh and also struck with the name of a moneyer, Raul Derling, alone. Smaller numbers are recorded from Berwick and Edinburgh (**41**). A hoard of crescent and pellet coins along with Tealby pennies (1158-80) was found in Dyke churchyard near Elgin and single finds have been made on a site in the High Street, Perth, and also at Kelso and Fala. With the exception of a few Stephen pennies in the Bute hoard, Tealby coins are the earliest post-Conquest English issue to be found in Scotland and single specimens have been unearthed at Jedburgh and Eyemouth.

Henry II's great re-coinage of 1180 resulted in the English short cross coinage. With the 'short' cross taking up only the centre of the reverse, its development and classes have been well plotted due to a wealth of documentary references in royal records. The surviving Scottish records of the period are almost totally silent as regards coinage and it is fortuitous that the two references which do exist note the start and finish of the Scottish short cross issue. The Chronicle of Melrose seems to indicate that it commenced in 1195 while the Scotichronicon records its replacement in 1250.

42 William I, short cross penny, phase A, 1195-1205, Edinburgh, Hue, [HVE:ONEDNEBVR].

The short cross pennies struck during this period can be grouped into five classes though the dates of each of these are somewhat vague. The obverse continues to depict a royal head in profile with the name and title of King William while on the reverse a central voided cross is surrounded by the name of the moneyer and his mint. In the first group, phase A, which lasted about a decade, the coins of the moneyer Raul at Roxburgh are most numerous. The mint at Perth was re-opened and Edinburgh also contributed (**42**). Perhaps about 1205, when a major re-coinage took place in England, phase B pennies appeared with the obverse form LE REI WILAM and generally without a mint name. The names of two moneyers are usually found on the reverse, especially those of Hue and Walter as HVE WALTER (**43**), and among the others the single name of Henri le Rus, occasionally with the addition of DE PERT, shows Perth was still active.

Although William I died in 1214, phase B pennies continued to be struck perhaps as late as 1230 when phase C pennies, bearing a bearded portrait, were introduced. Although these pieces still bear the name of

43 William I, short cross penny, phase B, 1205-30, struck by the moneyers Hue and Walter working together [hVEWALTER].

William, the portrait is similar to that on the next phase D coins with the name of Alexander. The introduction of coins in Alexander II's name took place about 1235 and Roxburgh continued to be the main mint though pennies in the names of joint moneyers still continued. A small number of short cross pennies with the name of Alexander but a beardless bust are assigned to the seven year old Alexander III who came to the throne in 1249. Most were struck at Berwick but unique examples are known from Glasgow, Perth and Roxburgh.

A small number of hoards throw some light on the circulation of the short cross penny in Scotland. The largest, which contained several hundred coins, was found at Tom A'Bhuraich, Aberdeenshire, and was composed mainly of English issues with some posthumous issues of William I. Concealed around 1240, it also included cut halfpennies and farthings. The hoard of twenty-six pieces unearthed during excavations at Dun Lagaidh, Ross and Cromarty, contains nine cut halfpennies, one of them a phase B Hue Walter issue. Similarly a hoard from Keith, Banffshire, of about 100 coins was mainly English in content and that from Dun Hiadin on Tiree contained no Scottish piece at all. The remaining three hoards from the south of Scotland are less well recorded but one from Badinsgill, Peeblesshire, was mainly Scottish.

Fortunately the picture presented by the hoards is greatly enhanced by groups or single finds from excavations as well as by other stray finds. Over twenty sites have yielded short cross material and in half of these the piece is cut, usually as a halfpenny, indicating some need for small change. The majority are English pieces, generally dating after the major re-coinage of 1205, but Scottish issues have come from a third of the sites and include a phase A cut farthing from Cambuskenneth Abbey, near Stirling. Many are from urban sites:

Cromarty, Aberdeen and Inverness in the north; Perth and St Andrews in the east; Glasgow and Lanark in the west; and Jedburgh in the borders. Holywood church, Dumfriesshire, has yielded over ten, not seemingly constituting a hoard, and others include a phase D of Alexander II found outside Berwick and a Henry III of England issue from the

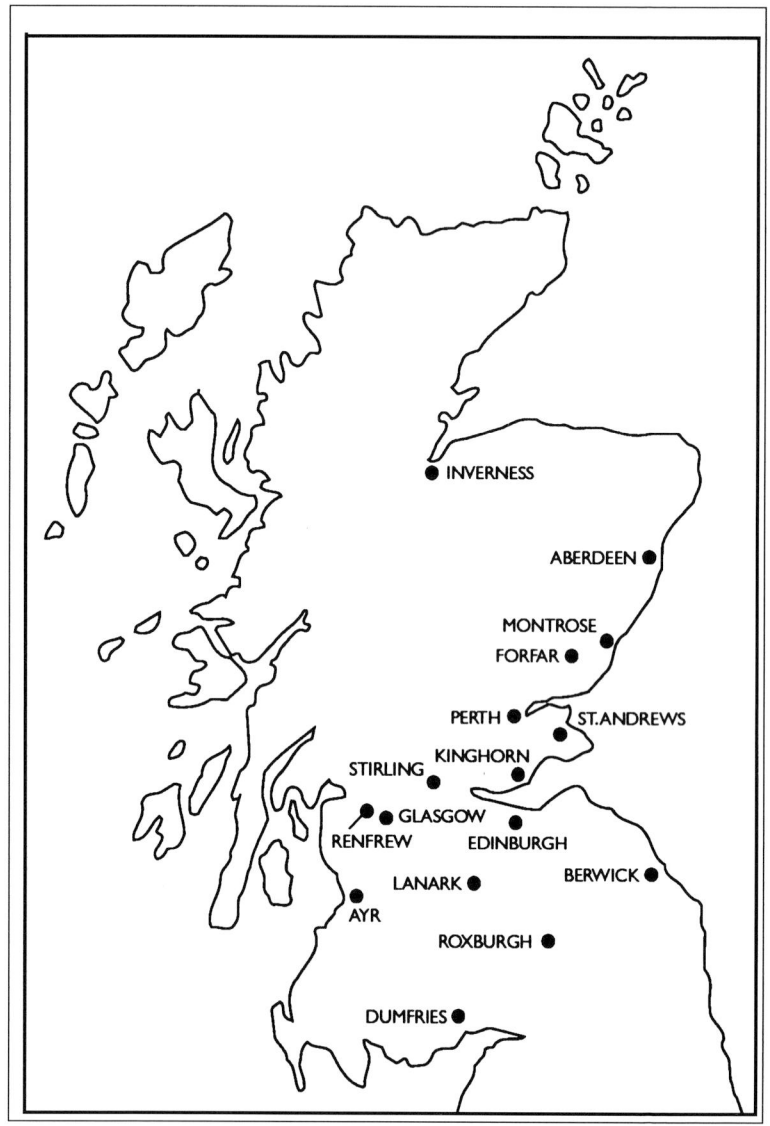

Fig. 3.1 Alexander III's long cross mints.

habitation site at The Udal on North Uist. The evidence of site finds and hoards thus suggests a great expansion in the use of coinage, including the extensive use of cut fractions, throughout Scotland, especially in the burghs, in the first half of the thirteenth century.

Despite an apparent demand for small change, only the penny was struck. However, the cross in the centre of the reverse, the short cross, was voided or double which provided a ready guide for the cutting of the penny into halves for halfpennies and fourths for farthings. The Scottish mints, like their English counterparts, were presumably responsible for the official provision of cut coins but no doubt much private cutting took place as the need arose. Cutting of another kind involving clipping of part or all of the edge of the penny was also common though quite illegal. The thinness of the coin and the softness of the silver made clipping easy and tempting and it was to remain a persistent problem throughout the Middle Ages. However, in an attempt to solve it, in 1247 Henry III introduced the long cross penny on which the cross was extended to the edge of the coin in the hope that clipping being then more obvious, it would be difficult to get away with and so would die out.

The idea was followed by Alexander III in 1250 when a Scottish long cross penny made its debut. This coinage is divided into eight classes based on the shape of the King's bust. Class I is merely transitional and it is with classes II and especially III that the main recoinage took place (**44-45**). Seven mints are named on the former but following the change of design to type III the number of mints increased to sixteen. These were located throughout the country to allow all with old coins to exchange to do so without difficulty and their number indicates a desire for thoroughness in the change-over.

44 Alexander III, long cross penny, class II, Glasgow, Walter, [WA/LT/ER'O/NG].

45 Alexander III, long cross penny, class III, Edinburgh, Alexander, [AL/EXO/NED/EN].

The north-east was served by Inverness, Aberdeen, Montrose and Forfar; further south there were mints at Perth, St Andrews, Stirling and Kinghorn; across the central belt Edinburgh, Glasgow, Renfrew and Lanark were in operation; and Ayr, Dumfries, Roxburgh and Berwick completed the operation. This was the largest and most comprehensive mint organization recorded for a re-coinage.

46 *Alexander III, long cross penny, class VII, Glasgow, Walter,*
[WA/LT/ERON/GLA].

Coins of classes IV, V and VI are rare and emanate from five, two and five mints respectively. Only Edinburgh issued all three and only rose to two moneyers for class V. These classes seem to represent further small strikings soon after the completion of the main re-coinage when the other mints presumably had already successfully finished their task. Class VII probably followed immediately and was a more substantial issue with eight mints operating (**46**), among which Berwick with four moneyers was the most important. Berwick again was the main mint for the final class VIII though with support from Roxburgh and Perth as in the previous class. It would appear that the whole process, covering the eight classes, was carried out in about five years, for coins of all classes were included in the main portion of the large hoard of coins found in Colchester in 1969. That main element is dated by the English coins to 1256. Only class VIII continues, for other varieties of it were found in the huge hoard hidden in Brussels a decade later and further strikings may have continued for some time after. The overwhelming number of Berwick coins would suggest that this was where most of the later long cross pennies of Alexander III were struck, though some activity also seems to have taken place at Roxburgh.

The names of over two dozen moneyers occur on the long cross pennies with, not surprisingly, seven connected with Berwick. There were four at each of the Aberdeen, Perth and Roxburgh mints and three at

Edinburgh. The remainder possessed one with occasionally a second and in some instances the one moneyer appears to have been responsible for a number of mints. Such is the case with Walter at Glasgow, Renfrew and Dumfries as well as Montrose while the same Wilam seems to have been active at Lanark and Kinghorn. Nothing is known of either of these men nor indeed of any of the long cross moneyers with the exception of John Cokin at Perth. He is likely to be the man of that same name who was a provost of Perth in the reign of Alexander II and therefore the sort of responsible person appointed as a moneyer.

The number of long cross pennies recovered from Scotland is, however, not large. The hoard found at Hazelrigg, Dumfriesshire, contained about 100 coins most of them English and suggesting a date of concealment about 1270. The small find of fourteen from Newcastleton, Roxburghshire, were all English and seemingly early in the series while a little group of a penny and three cut halfpennies from the Glenluce Sands, Wigtownshire, was also English. The details of a further four hoards, none large, are really too vague even to be certain that they did consist of long cross coins.

Again the pattern of circulation is better shown by the record of groups and single finds. Over a dozen sites have yielded long cross issues, half of which include or consist of cut halfpennies. Apart from a cut halfpenny of Roxburgh found at Cambuskenneth Abbey, English coins predominate. Inchaffrey Abbey, Perthshire, has also produced several long cross coins but most come from urban sites. Four pennies and four cut halfpennies have been found on the presumed medieval fair site at the Castlegate in Cromarty and others have come from Aberdeen, Forfar, Perth, Stirling, Rutherglen and Ayr. Again the use of coinage seems widespread in the period 1250 -1280 and the high proportion of cut coins shows the extensive use of fractions. However, it is surprising that, though the long cross constituted a large and major re-coinage, fewer finds have survived than from the previous short cross issue and those that do are greatly outnumbered by their English counterparts. Die studies suggest the Scottish long cross was approximately four times as large as the short cross coinage and, though there were thirty years – compared to the fifty-five for the short cross – for these to be lost, or hoarded and not recovered, this hardly explains the discrepancy.

Their replacement in 1280 was struck in even larger numbers and it survives as the most common of Scottish medieval coins. The new coins are well struck with a good portrait on the obverse and now a long single cross on the reverse, as on the English type intoduced a year

47 *Alexander III, second coinage, 1280-86, penny, with neat hair, and four mullets of six points giving twenty-four points on the reverse.*

48 *Alexander III, second coinage, halfpenny.*

49 *Alexander III, second coinage, farthing.*

earlier. For the first time the king is given his full title, King of Scots. The inscription, ALEXANDER DEI GRA[TIA] REX SCOTORUM, thus takes up both sides of the coin leaving no room for the name of the mint. A single cross replaced the double voided cross for there was no longer any need of a guide for cutting. Round halfpennies and farthings were intoduced at this time and are of the same types as the penny (**47-49**).

The absence of a mint name makes the classification of the single long cross coins somewhat difficult and this is not helped by the continuing lack of documentary references. Despite the large number struck, it is likely that most belong to the early 1280s. There may have been some further minting until the end of the reign in 1286 but it is very uncertain whether any appeared later than this. It has been estimated that the total issue may have amounted to as many as 50 million pennies. The surviving coins have received detailed analysis and fall into two main groups based on the shape of the bust, the first with a small neat head with tidy hair and the second with more bushy hair sweeping backwards (**50**). Sub-groups can be identified on the basis of lettering and other details, but it is a complicated system.

50 Alexander III, second coinage, penny, with swept hair, and two mullets of six points and two stars of seven points giving twenty-six points.

A further method of grouping is to be found within the arms of the cross on the reverse. In each quarter is a mullet with either five or six points or a star of seven points and various combinations of these in the four quarters of the coin lead to a total of points ranging from twenty to twenty-eight. The interpretation of this points system of nine groups is uncertain. It does not readily tie in with other features and does not appear to have any chronological significance. The fact that there are a large number of coins with twenty-four points (from four mullets of six points) and mainly associated with the neater hair has led to the suggestion that these were struck at Berwick which is likey to have continued as the main mint. However, it has proved more difficult to assign mints to the other eight groups though Edinburgh may be represented by twenty points (from four mullets of five points) and St Andrews by twenty-two points (two mullets of five points and two of six). In any event such a major re-coinage carried out over a short period of time must have required at least nine mints when compared with the number for that of 1250.

51 *John Baliol (1292-6), rough issue, penny.*

52 *John Baliol, smooth issue, penny.*

Once established the new penny was to have a long life, appearing as part of the currency for almost a century. Similar issues appeared under subsequent monarchs. John Baliol, despite a short reign from 1292 to 1296, produced two issues. The earlier of these is known as the 'rough' issue from the crude appearance of the head and lettering while the later, much better designed and struck, is termed the 'smooth' issue (**51-52**). On both occasions the penny was accompanied by a halfpenny only. Most, with the anonymous REX SCOTORUM reverse, were probably struck at Berwick but some of both issues bear CIVITAS SANDRE for St Andrews. There is some documentary evidence that the Bishop of St Andrews had been given the right to coin money, though of the same type as the king's. The privilege was more of prestige than profit. With the loss of Berwick to the English in 1296 it is unlikely any more coins of John were struck.

There appears to have been a gap of over twenty years before a further issue appeared but supply in the form of Alexander III and imported Edwardian pence, brought in perhaps mainly by the English invaders, seems to have been adequate. It was only after the success of Bannockburn in 1314 and the re-capture of Berwick in 1318 that Robert Bruce issued his own coinage. Apart from bearing the name

53 Robert I, penny, about 1320.

54 Robert I, halfpenny.

55 Robert I, farthing.

ROBERTUS, these pennies continue the previous REX SCOTORUM type and are of good appearance (**53**). It appears to have been a small coinage of short duration struck about 1320 and though fractions were included, Robert I's halfpence and farthings are very rare (**54-55**). In 1329 he was succeeded by his son, David II, for whom a small coinage of halfpennies and some farthings was struck in the early 1330s until the capture of Berwick by Edward III. The absence of pennies mirrors the situation in England where few pennies were struck at this time. It was to be the middle of the century before coins were struck once more, probably in Edinburgh. Though David was a prisoner in English hands,

56 David II, penny, 1350-57.

pennies bearing his name were struck in some numbers between 1351 and 1357 (**56**). The King regained his freedom in 1357 and returned home to usher in soon afterwards a new era in the coinage.

The number of hoards containing long single cross pennies now exceeds a hundred, several of which are of considerable size. In particular there is a group of six such finds from Aberdeen including the 1886 Upperkirkgate hoard of over 12,000 pennies and the 1983 and 1984 St Nicholas Street treasure troves of 4,493 and 2,538 pieces respectively. Another large find of about 9,000 coins was made at Montrave, Fifeshire, in 1877. Hoards of over 2,000 coins have been recovered at Parton and Carsphairn, both in Kirkcudbrightshire, and Duns Castle, Berwickshire, while smaller ones of note include the 1963 Renfrew find of 674 coins mainly put together about 1300 but with a small addition of pennies, halfpennies and farthings before final concealment around 1321 and important for suggesting a date slightly before for the striking of Robert I's coinage.

Despite the size of some of these finds, especially in relation to other Scottish coin hoards, it has already been pointed out that the fourteenth century value of them – for example about £50 for the Upperkirkgate find – is not great and that such sums were not unusual then for merchants or revenue collectors. The main contents of the hoards are English pennies which provided the bulk of the coinage in circulation in Scotland at that time. Large as Alexander III's output was, Scottish coins usually amount to less than 3% of the hoards: 126 coins or 2.8% of Aberdeen 1983 and 67 coins or 2.6% of Aberdeen 1984. For a short time around 1300 continental coins featured in the hoards probably due to the strict ban then imposed on them in England, thus bringing some northwards. Otherwise several hoards seem to belong to the 1330s and may be associated with the attempt of

Edward Baliol to take the throne. Two groups seem to belong to this period of unrest, one hidden in the south-west and the second in the north-east between Perth and Aberdeen. The Upperkirkgate hoard may actually be associated with the sack of Aberdeen in 1336 by the English. However, the two more recent Aberdeen hoards have been assigned to the middle of the 1340s and provide evidence of continuing prosperity despite the recent devastation.

It is surprising, however, that Aberdeen has yielded no single find of Edwardian sterlings with the exception of two from a trial excavation in Loch Street. Otherwise the single long cross penny is a frequent find throughout Scotland with over fifty sites recorded. No less than twenty-two have been found in the vicinity of Inchaffrey Abbey and eight were recovered during excavation of St. John's Tower in Ayr. As with the hoards most are English, but some Scottish issues do turn up such as the penny of Alexander III from Linlithgow Friary and one of John Baliol from Urquhart Castle. Very few fractions have been recovered but a halfpenny of Alexander was found at Inchaffrey Abbey and a farthing at the Meal Vennel site in Perth. Such pennies continued to circulate until the middle of the century and, despite major changes to the coinage by David II in 1357, the Alexandrian and Edwardian coins were so numerous that it was not until the 1370s that they finally ceased to constitute an element of the currency.

CHAPTER FOUR
The Silver Groat 1350-1550

David II instituted a major re-coinage in 1357, the major feature of which was the introduction of a larger silver coin worth fourpence. The groat was to play a central role for the next 200 years. Increasing trade in Europe in the thirteenth century had resulted in the widespread appearance of such a more convenient piece and it had at last been successfully adopted in England in 1351. At that time David was a prisoner of his brother-in-law, Edward III, and would have become familiar with the new coins. His release in 1357 and the need for a re-coinage presented an ideal opportunity to bring about change.

The design on the obverse continues to be a profile bust of the king, though within a tressure, and the larger space available permitted a more pleasing image than that found on the earlier, smaller pennies. Space also allowed the king's title to be included on this side. The reverse design remained essentially as before, a cross with a mullet in each angle, but now with two inscriptions because of the greater space. The outer, which was to remain unchanged for two centuries, is taken from the Psalms, DOMINUS PROTECTOR ET LIBERATOR MEUS ('The Lord is my defender and redeemer'). The inner gives the name of the mint. There is now a system of small privy marks designed to give greater control over an issue. These are numerous and complicated but a good example is the appearance of a small D in various quarters of the reverse of one group (**57**). This may stand for David or perhaps Donatus Mulekyn, one of the engravers. The groats were struck with a fineness of .925 silver and a weight of 72 grains [4.67 grams] as in England and they were freely interchangeable like the pennies in previous reigns. A halfgroat (**58**) was also struck as were pennies.

David II's second coinage was a large one struck over ten years. It is classified according to the shape of the bust, of which there are four main types – A to D. The earliest, bust A, is a small youthful head (**59**) replaced by a larger, but still young and not unpleasing, bust B (**60**). An older image, bust C, may perhaps be simply described as ugly (**61**). Bust D makes the King look as if he is wearing a mask (**62**). A similar bust was used throughout the next reign and has engendered the term 'Robert II bust' for the final representation of David II. Edinburgh was

THE SILVER GROAT 1350-1550

57 David II, heavy groat, with D in one angle of the reverse.

58 David II, heavy coinage, 1357-67, halfgroat, group A, Aberdeen.

59 David II, heavy coinage, groat, group A, Edinburgh.

60 David II, heavy coinage, groat, group B, Aberdeen.

61 David II, heavy coinage, groat, group C, Edinburgh.

62 David II, heavy coinage, groat, group D, Edinburgh.

the main mint but in the earlier part of the coinage Aberdeen also produced coins with busts A and B.

In 1367 the weight of the groat was reduced to 61.5 grains. David's 'light' groats continue to bear the 'Robert II' head but can be distinguished by the presence of a star on the sceptre (**63**). All groats, half-groats and pennies (**64**) of this third coinage were struck at Edinburgh. Four years later Robert II succeeded his uncle but, apart from the change in name, the types remained similar (**65-68**). Again this is a

63 David II, light coinage, 1367-71, groat, Edinburgh.

64 David II, light coinage, 1367-71, penny, Edinburgh.

THE SILVER GROAT 1350-1550

65 Robert II (1371-90), groat, Edinburgh.

66 Robert II (1371-90), halfgroat, Edinburgh.

67 Robert II (1371-90), penny Edinburgh.

68 Robert II (1371-90), halfpenny, Edinburgh.

large issue still awaiting full classification. Edinburgh remained the main mint but others were opened at Perth and, on a smaller scale, at Dundee. Many of Robert's coins have a small B behind the head presumably standing for Bonagio of Florence, the moneyer responsible for their issue.

It is with the coinages of David II and Robert II that references begin to appear in the Scottish records. Charters were granted early in 1357 to Adam Tor appointing him as Warden in charge of the administration of the proposed coinage and to James Mulekyn as Master Moneyer to be in charge of its production. Tor, who was a burgess of Edinburgh, rendered accounts to the King for most years from 1357 to 1364 and it is these which in turn mention the other moneyers, Donatus Mulekyn and Bonagio. The latter worked at the Durham mint between 1358 and 1363 and seems to have been employed in Edinburgh from about 1364 where he was still recorded as a moneyer as late as 1393. An Act of Parliament of 1366 ordered a new coinage with a 'signum notabile' or special mark to distinguish it from previous similar issues and, taken with another Act of the following year ordering a reduction in weight, seems to refer to the 'light' coinage of 1367 with the star. The latter Act also ordered that seven out of the 352 pennies coined from each pound of silver should go to the King as seignorage – a profit of about 2% of the face value of the whole issue. The records also suggest that the mint in Edinburgh was housed in a building belonging to one John Corry and situated in the High Street next to St Giles.

The records indicate a large output from 1357 to 1390 and this is borne out by hoards and other finds. A few vaguely recorded hoards suggest groats of Edward III were reaching Scotland soon after their introduction in 1351 but even in the 1360s the earlier pennies predominate as in huge hoards from Closeburn, Dumfriesshire, and Montrave in Fife. Both, however, contained a number of the new coins. The Montrave find, hidden about 1365, consisted of over 9,000 pennies accompanied by 127 groats and 7 halfgroats of David II and 39 groats and 4 halfgroats of Edward III. Among the Scottish pieces 4 were of Aberdeen and the rest of Edinburgh.

Two hoards concealed in the 1370s show the number of pennies decreasing and the groat becoming more common. That from Aberdour, Fife, seems to be mainly a hoard of the previous decade to which has been added a few coins of Robert II. Among its 295 coins, over 200 were sterlings, or pennies, and of 25 groats and 12 halfgroats, 19 and 10 respectively were of David II's heavy issue. Aberdour seems to be the earlier of the two discoveries, both probably hidden by 1375.

THE SILVER GROAT 1350-1550

The second, from Tranent, East Lothian, contained 150 coins of which 60 were sterlings struck before 1335. In addition there were 2 groats and 1 halfgroat of Edward III, but the majority of the larger pieces belonged to David II and Robert II. These included 7 heavy groats and 4 light groats of the former and 14 groats of the latter. There were 9 halfgroats of each monarch and among the issues of Robert II present there were twice as many coins of Perth as of Edinburgh, which suggests a date about or soon after 1375.

The sterlings and Edwardian groats seem to have disappeared entirely by 1380 and a small group of finds, none containing more than a hundred coins, consist essentially of Scottish issues with those of Robert II outnumbering David II and apparently concealed during the 1380s. Among recorded single finds early groats and halfgroats are few, perhaps because, if dropped, they were easier to recover than the smaller penny or more likely, being more valuable, they were more diligently searched for. There are few of Edward III or David II but single stray finds of Robert II are not uncommon. Groats and halfgroats seem to occur in equal numbers and the mint, when recorded, is more often Edinburgh than Perth for both denominations.

By the end of the fourteenth century the silver coinage appears to have been dominated by the issues of Robert III. Although Robert ascended the throne in 1390, the earliest documentary evidence for this reign is an Act of Parliament passed at Perth in 1393. A gold coinage was introduced, while the fineness of pennies and halfpennies was reduced. There were two major changes in the fine silver coinage. The weight of the groat was reduced to just over 46 grains and, more obviously, the King's bust became full face. The norm in respect of the royal image on the coinage for over 250 years had been a profile bust with sceptre. Now it was depicted in the usual English fashion, and in a further copying of southern style the mullets on the reverse were replaced by groups of three pellets. This may have been intended to make them more acceptable in England but the reduced weight greatly affected their exchange value. These changes were introduced by Robert, Duke of Albany, the King's younger brother and Governor of Scotland. Although baptised John, the King took up the name Robert for his title and being in poor health left the running of his realm to Albany.

The coinage commenced with Edinburgh alone striking groats with a rather crude bust of poor style. This first issue can also be distinguished by the presence of a group of three small pellets on the cusps of the tressure, hitherto plain, around the bust (**69**). Halfgroats, pennies and halfpennies were also produced. Subsequently the style of

THE SILVER GROAT 1350-1550

69 *Robert III, heavy coinage, 1390-1403, groat, with pellets on cusps, Edinburgh.*

70 *Robert III, heavy coinage, 1390-1403, groat, with trefoils on cusps, Edinburgh.*

bust improved to a neater appearance and was accompanied by a change to a trefoil on the cusps (**70**). Coins of this second issue were struck at Perth (**71**) and Aberdeen as well as at Edinburgh. These two issues constitute Robert III's 'heavy' coinage, for towards the end of the reign a further weight reduction to about 28 grains was introduced, perhaps about 1403. The 'light' groat is of the same type as its predecessor though the bust is not so well executed (**72**). This later coinage consists only of groats struck at Edinburgh, Aberdeen and now Dumbarton. This is the only occasion a mint operated at Dumbarton and, if situated in the castle, may have been opened after this had been recovered by the Crown in 1402.

The largest and most important hoard of this reign was found at Fortrose and contained over 1,000 groats of Robert's heavy coinage only, including fifty forgeries and some Perth coins overstruck on earlier groats of Robert II. Since no light groats were included, it appears to have been hidden about 1400. The inclusion of some Dumbarton groats in hoards from Edinburgh and Balgony Farm, Perthshire, indicate a

71 Robert III, heavy halfpenny, Perth.

72 Robert III, light coinage, 1403-06, groat, Edinburgh.

mixture of heavy and light groats and therefore a slightly later date of deposit. The latter find included halfgroats and some gold. A small hoard of about thirty unspecified groats of Robert III was unearthed on Killichonate Farm, Inverness-shire. Few single finds of coins of Robert III seem to have been made but a light groat of Edinburgh was found at Cambuskenneth Abbey and a heavy halfgroat of Perth was recovered during excavations at Leckie Broch, Stirlingshire.

There then follows something of a hiatus for about twenty years. There is a lack of documentary evidence, a lack of recorded coin finds and no strikings except probably of some pennies and halfpennies. Robert III's issues continued to circulate and presumably in sufficient numbers. This period also saw the continuation of Robert, Duke of Albany's government though now as Regent. Robert III had died in 1306 but his son, James I, was a prisoner in England. He was not released until 1424, on the promise of a £40,000 ransom.

James I was crowned at Scone in May 1424 and within a week Parliament passed an Act at Perth concerning a new coinage. It would

73 James I, fleur-de-lis groat, first variety, 1424, Edinburgh.

74 James I, fleur-de-lis groat, second variety, Edinburgh.

appear that a major re-coinage was undertaken soon after. The new groat, while retaining the facing bust, is of a quite different style and now bears a sceptre while in two of the angles on the reverse the groups of three pellets are replaced by a lis. This 'fleur-de-lis' groat was to be struck well into the next reign and although very numerous is divided into four main classes. Group I is by far the largest and probably represents the main part of the re-coinage (**73**). It is distinguished by a tall, neat, though uninspired, bust. The stops in the legends are composed of lis and saltires and there is a bewildering variety of privy marks mainly placed on and around the bust. The early fleur-de-lis groats were struck at Edinburgh, Perth and Linlithgow. These three mints, with the addition of Stirling, struck the second variety, group II, differing in having a much larger crown on the bust and with an annulet common among the stops and marks (**74**). It is now thought that this group was still in production when the murder of James I in 1437 set his seven year old son on the throne as James II.

THE SILVER GROAT 1350-1550

Accounts rendered by the Master Moneyer, Robert Gray, in 1434 and 1435 at Linlithgow and Stirling respectively still exist in the Exchequer Rolls. This was the only coinage to which Linlithgow contributed and the mint there was probably connected with the building of the great Renaissance palace for the King. It was ready for residence by mid-1434, hence the rendering of Gray's account there. The mint was situated, not in the palace, but near the Kirkstile in an apparently rented property of one John Ker, who had recently died. The mint in Edinburgh continued to be beside St. Giles though rent was now being paid to a new owner, Robert Nudry. In the 1440s the mint at Stirling was in a property rented from Robert Hakate.

75 *James II, fleur-de-lis groat, third variety, 1437-51, Edinburgh.*

The third variety of fleur-de-lis groat, group III, probably commenced about 1440 though it was not struck at Perth and only in small numbers at Linlithgow and Stirling (75). The crown on this is tall and narrow whereas on the fourth variety, group IV, the crown possesses a large central fleur and the bust is draped. This final group was not large and was confined to Edinburgh. The first recorded Trial of the Pyx in Scotland took place on 19 July 1438 when samples put aside for testing by the Master Moneyer, Robert Gray, and the Warden, Thomas de Cranston, were found by the Commissioners in Edinburgh to be good and lawful. Throughout its issue from 1424 to 1451 the fleur-de-lis groat weighed about 36 grains compared to the 60 grains to which the English groat had been reduced in 1412. No halfgroats were struck throughout this period. Edinburgh was largely responsible for the pennies and halfpennies now being struck in much debased silver only. There appears to be no well recorded hoard of fleur-de-lis groats and single finds are very few.

It was to be October 1451 before Parliament set out regulations for a new coinage. The basic types remained unchanged but the sceptre was removed and on the reverse the lis were replaced by crowns. These 'crown and pellets' groats of James II were on the whole somewhat better produced (**76**). They were also to be of the same weight as the English groat and at 58.9 grains were indeed only very slightly short of the 60 grains groat in circulation in England. However, the new groat was intended to pass at eightpence in Scotland and in fact seems to have circulated at twelve pence, which was declared its official tariff in a further Act of 1456. There was a small and short first issue with a draped bust before the main coinage got underway. This second issue is very large and the three main groups are distinguished by the shape of the crown, the initial and privy marks and the lettering. Edinburgh struck all the classes of which the third is the most numerous. For this last group mints were opened at Aberdeen and Stirling (**77-78**) and small numbers of now very rare groats were struck at Roxburgh and Perth. Some halfgroats were also struck. The coins of Roxburgh are probably associated with the seige of 1460 at which James II was killed by the accidental explosion of a cannon. However, the crown and pellet groats continued to be struck during the early years of his successor, including the very rare fourth group.

76 *James II, crown and pellets groat, 1451-60, Edinburgh.*

77 *James II, crown and pellets groat, 1451-60, Aberdeen.*

78 *James II, crown and pellets groat, 1451-60, Stirling.*

79 James III, mullet groat (group I), 1467, Edinburgh.

80 James III, mullet groat (group I), 1467, Berwick.

It was not until about 1467 that a new coinage was struck for James III and from then until the end of his reign in 1488 five different types of groat were issued. Three of these are of the conventional facing bust type and two are quite novel in bearing more realistic portraits. The main new feature of the conventional groats (groups I, III and IV) is the use of mullets instead of the crowns on the reverse. The earliest mullet (of six points) groats comprising group I were struck at Edinburgh and Berwick (**79-80**). Still tariffed at twelve pence, they were reduced in weight to just over 39 grains – somewhat below the new English weight of 48 grains introduced in 1464 by Edward IV. It was as a result of the Yorkist victories of 1461 that the Lancastrian Henry VI became a refugee at the Scottish court and it was he who then handed over Berwick to the Scots. Some of the groats from both mints bear the initials T and L of Thomas Tod and Alexander Livingstoun whose moneyers' accounts for 1476 and 1478 are still extant. Some of the very rare halfgroats are notable for bearing the numeral 3 after the King's name, the first instance of such a designation on the Scottish coinage.

Group I mullet groats were replaced by group III, still with six points, in 1475. Again Edinburgh and Berwick were the only mints.

81 James III, light mullet groat (group IV), Edinburgh.

The English regained Berwick in 1482 so the third, and largest, issue of the mullet groats (IV), now with five points, along with their halfgroats and fine silver pennies, was confined to Edinburgh (**81**). The rare group V mullet groats are believed to have been struck in 1488 by the King's opponents.

82 James III, first portrait groat (group II), 1471-83, Edinburgh.

In stark contrast to these competent but mundane mullet groats are the two issues of James III's portrait groats (II and VI). They are remarkable for their early appearance and laudable for their attempt to achieve a more realistic portrait of the monarch. The earlier seems to have been quite a large issue, from Edinburgh alone, and depicts a young King – then about 30 – clothed and facing half right (**82**). Of note too is the introduction of thistle heads on the reverse which bears only one legend giving the mint name. Such pieces were struck between 1471 and 1483 and it perhaps detracts from them that the silver was debased to a fineness of .770.

THE SILVER GROAT 1350-1550

83 James III, second portrait groat (group VI), 1484-8, Edinburgh.

The second portrait groat of 1484 to 1488, however, returned to normal fineness and at just over 47 grains very nearly equalled the weight of the English groat though it circulated at fourteen pence. This portrait is perhaps the more realistic and shows James facing half left (**83**). They were struck mainly in Edinburgh with some from Aberdeen, perhaps in connection with the King's visit there in 1488. This was the last occasion that a mint was in operation there. It is unfortunate that the low relief of both portraits means they are now usually found somewhat rubbed and flat. Good examples, however, show their charm and style. This is not to underestimate their importance for when the Renaissance interest in the human being was still only beginning to find expression in coin portraiture in Italy, here alone far to the north the idea was being put into practice by James III.

It is a pity that James IV did not continue with a Renaissance image but rather throughout his reign, from 1488 until 1513, reverted to the use of the old stylized full-face bust. An Act of Parliament of 1488 ordered a new coinage and until about 1496 this consisted of a 'heavy' issue groat of just over 47 grains current at fourteen pence (**84**). Two

84 James IV, heavy groat, 1489-96, without numeral.

groups are recognized, with crowns in two of the reverse angles on the earlier and with one crown replaced by a lis on the later. Around 1496 the weight was reduced to just over 39 grains for a 'light' groat to circulate at twelve pence (85). On both issues James is frequently indicated as the fourth king of that name (86-88). Groats and halfgroats were struck throughout the reign and silver pennies (tariffed at threepence) in the light issue only. Edinburgh was the sole mint.

The number of hoards recorded rises again for the latter half of the the fifteenth century and a score are known whose dates of deposit range from the 1460s to around the turn of the century. In the 1460s they seem to have consisted mainly of English silver such as the find from Bridge of Don, Aberdeen, made up of 197 groats of which 192 ranged from Edward III to the light issue of Edward IV intoduced in 1464. During the next twenty years Scottish coins seem to predominate though often with an admixture of gold or billon. A hoard of groats from Kilmarnock was entirely composed of James III coins of his first portrait and late mullets issues. A little hoard from near Edinburgh consisted of four of these first portrait groats and three billon placks of James III, while a bag found in the ruins of Perth Castle contained an unspecified number of silver and billon coins of James III and IV. The Dunscore, Dumfriesshire, hoard contained seventy billon coins, mainly pennies, along with seven English and six Scottish groats no later than 1484. However, although a major element of the Glen Afton hoard was 41 gold coins from James I to III, the majority of the contents were over 100 English groats and halfgroats.

In the last decade of the century and early years after 1500 the mixture of metals becomes more pronounced. Only the Ayr find is all of silver, 106 Scottish to James IV against 29 English groats and halfgroats. The discoveries at St Andrews and Whitburn are essentially of silver with Scottish issues in greater numbers in both. However, the hoards from Rhoneston, Dumfriesshire, and Glenluce, Wigtownshire, hidden respectively about 1490 and 1495, each contained only a small percentage of silver coin and a large number of billon pennies. A large discovery at Perth consisted of 18 gold coins, 611 silver and 499 billon coins. Among the English coins present, from Edward III to Edward IV and all worn and clipped, halfgroats predominated. Scottish silver was somewhat more numerous ending with James IV and including many fleur-de-lis groats. It was the latter, current at sixpence or half the twelve pence of the James IV groats, along with the older English halfgroats which made up for the insufficient numbers of Scottish halfgroats. The placks in the Perth find show an increasing tendency towards a greater use of billon and the mixture of metals, unusual theo-

85 *James IV, light groat, 1496-1513, without numeral.*

86 *James IV, light groat, 1496-1513, with* QRA.

87 *James IV, light groat, 1496-1513, with IIII.*

88 *James IV, light groat, 1496-1513, with medieval 4.*

retically where hoards tend to be of the one metal and usually the best available, suggests people were glad to have any precious metal coin to add to their savings.

Little or no silver seems to have been struck in the latter part of James IV's reign, but the twelvepenny groats used for the Royal Maundy gifts were perhaps always new strikings, and certainly so in 1512, when a new type showed the King with a beard. The coinage struck immediately after James V's reign began in 1513 consisted only of gold and billon. It was not until 1526 that a silver coinage was ordered to be struck with a groat, reduced to a fineness of .833, to pass at eighteen pence. The Master Moneyer was to be James Achesoun who in October of the same year was given a second contract slightly reducing the seignorage paid to the King. However, a year later a German miner, Joachim Hochstetter, was given the sole right to strike silver coin for ten years. There is no evidence that this contract was ever carried out and it would appear that a Hochstetter issue does not exist. Achesoun is named in the accounts for 1530, 1531 and 1536 and was still in office when the second coinage came to an end in 1538.

Portraiture returned with the second coinage groats of James V. The King is shown in profile, wearing a fur mantle over a tunic, in the style adopted on the English coinage late in the reign of Henry VII and continued by Henry VIII after his accession in 1509 (**89**). It was a style familiar in European coinages of the later fifteenth century. On the reverse of James's groat a shield bearing the lion rampant is superimposed on a large cross and there is a single legend naming the sole mint in operation, Edinburgh. On the earliest group the word VILLA is used to describe the city, while on the later groups OPPIDUM appears. Four groups are distinguished by a different bust and the stops used in the legends. Groups I and II (**90**) may be the products of Achesoun's two early contracts, while the largest, group III, may account for most of the issues after that (**91**). The final group, IV, is accompanied by a fairly large issue of one-third groats bearing a similar, rather youngish portrait and perhaps struck in the later 1530s (**92**).

Hoards from the early decades of the sixteenth century, especially of silver, continue to be scarce. A large, but vaguely recorded, hoard of gold and silver from Eddleston, Peeblesshire, may be dated to this period by the inclusion of a gold coin of James V. A find from Mauchline, Ayrshire, contained forty-five English groats and halfgroats to Henry VIII and forty-nine Scottish coins to James IV. It also included a small group of billon coins, one a plack of James V, and may have been concealed around 1520. Two hoards, discovered at Clifton, West Lothian, and at Jedburgh, both appear to have contained several hundred silver coins, including issues of Henry VIII and James V. A group III groat of James V helps date the concealment of the hoard , mainly of billon placks, discovered at Linlithgow to about 1530. Stray finds of groats of James IV and V seem virtually non-existent.

The issues of James V between 1526 and 1538 are the last silver groats of the series. They were put into circulation at eighteen pence in considerable contrast to the first groats of 1357 issued at fourpence, a figure still held by the English groat in 1526. In 1357 Scottish and

THE SILVER GROAT 1350-1550

89 James V, second coinage, 1526-38, groat, type I.

90 James V, second coinage, 1526-38, groat, type II.

91 James V, second coinage 1526-38, groat, type III.

92 James V, second coinage 1526-38, one third groat, type IV.

English groats were similar, except in design, and the following year David II sought of Edward III and was granted interchangeability as with the previous coinages of pennies. Yet in 1367 David reduced the weight of his groat resulting in its being accepted for only threepence in England, and this was reduced to twopence in 1390. Further reduction in weight by Robert III in 1393 brought about abandonment by the government of the fiction that Scottish coins were equivalent to sterling, and the term 'usual money of Scotland' replaced sterling in

Table 4.1 Comparison of Scottish and English Groats

Date	tariff	weight	fineness	Eng. 4d .925	ratio
1357	4d	72gr	.925	72gr	1:1
1367	4d	61.5gr	.925		4:3
1390	4d	46gr	.925		2:1
1403	4d	28gr	.925		
1424	6d	36gr	.925	60gr (1412)	
1451	12d	59gr	.925		3:1
1471	6d	34gr	.770	48gr (1464)	
1475	12d	39gr	.925		
1484	14d	47gr	.925		
1496	12d	39gr	.925		
1526	18d	42gr	.883	42.75 (1526)	4:1

royal documents. In due course values, wages and prices were given in pounds, shillings and pence Scots.

Such debasement by lowering the weight, and later by raising the face value, of the groat was to recur throughout the medieval period in Scotland. However, some of the change was unavoidably due to depreciation. The price of gold and silver rose steadily and, unless a coin had its weight reduced or its value increased, it would become more valuable than its official rate and disappear into the melting pot. Equally, silver would be too dear to obtain for coining at the old tariffs. England reacted to such probems in 1412, 1464 and 1526. Debasement in its more common form of increasing the amount of alloy, used to harden the relatively soft precious metal for the wear and tear of circulation, was also used in Scotland, though rarely on the groat. This was struck in .925 silver except for the first portrait issue of James III at .700 fine and the 1526 issue of James V at .880 fine. However, the penny was debased in this way, at first by Robert III and then as a matter of course by the Jameses. The amount of precious metal in these debased or billon coins varied greatly but they remained pennies. This meant that the groat had to be revalued upwards in turn effecting a devaluation against its English counterpart. Occasionally silver pennies were still struck as in 1496 but they circulated at a higher value, threepence in this instance. The issue of a billon penny opened the way for the striking of other billon coins such as the plack.

Debasement, depreciation, revaluation and devaluation thus all affected the medieval coinage of Scotland but they should not necessarily be viewed in a negative sense. The appearance of smaller value coins was undoubtedly useful in the provision of small change for minor transactions. Scotland was in fact in line with Europe while the stronger currency of England was the oddity. However, the respective policies were no doubt what was best suited to each side of the border.

CHAPTER FIVE
Gold in Medieval Scotland

During the course of the thirteenth century Europe had returned to a bi-metallic system of coinage in gold and silver. Edward III successfully introduced a gold coinage in England in 1351 and again this would have been familiar to David II. David's second major innovation in his re-coinage of 1357 was the striking of a gold coin.

The gold noble is very similar to its English prototype except for the king's name and title and the lion rampant appearing on the shield held by the king standing in the ship. This is the first appearance of the lion rampant on the coinage though it only became a prominent type from the end of the fourteenth century on the gold and not until the sixteenth century on the silver. The reverse of the noble has an elaborate cross with crowned lions in the angles and the legend, IESUS AUTEM TRANSIENS PER MEDIUM ILLORUM IBAT ('But Jesus, passing through the midst of them, went His way'). Again this is the first of a great variety of biblical quotations to be found on the reverses of the gold coins. The noble was equal to eighty pence or six shillings and eightpence or a half merk, the merk being the main unit of account. It was over 23 carats or 96% fine (**93**).

93 *David II, noble, 1357.*

Only four of these nobles are known to be extant. Such a low survival rate might suggest a small coinage which, if experimental, might be the case. Perhaps it was intended to pay off the ransom of 100,000 merks negotiated on David's release in 1357. Some national pride may have been salvaged by paying some or all of the instalments in Scottish gold coins. Once delivered, these would have been restruck into English nobles. On the other hand, a proclamation of 1372 prohibited the receipt of Scottish gold or silver coin in England except as bullion. This must refer to David's nobles. Only one is recorded with a findspot, in fact in Northumberland, while a few vague hoard reports suggest that nobles of Edward III constituted the bulk of whatever gold circulated north of the border up to about 1390. However, a Scottish Act of Parliament passed in 1385 set up new rates for the noble as well as a number of French and Flemish gold pieces thus showing perhaps a more mixed gold currency than discernible from the hoards alone.

David's noble did not herald a regular gold coinage and Robert II reverted to the issue of silver only. It was not until the accession of Robert III in 1390 that gold was reintroduced as a normal feature of the coinage. Although Robert's groats became unexpectedly anglicized in type, he turned to France for the model for his gold. The coin referred to in the later Act of Parliament of 1393 as 'a piece called the lion' copies the écu à la couronne of Charles VI. The obverse type is a crowned shield with the lion rampant while the reverse depicts the national saint, St Andrew, on his saltire cross with a lis on either side. The Latin inscription reads, 'Christ rules, Christ conquers, Christ commands' (**94**). A second smaller issue possesses a smaller crown and shield, and both are accompanied by halves or demi-lions with a crown over the shield but only the cross, without the saint, on the reverse (**95**).

The lion, struck 'de bono auro' or almost pure gold, was to weigh approximately 61.5 grains and to be current for five shillings. However, on the introduction of the light coinage about 1403, the weight fell to about 38 grains for the lions (**96**) and 20 grains for the demi-lions though a certain amount of variation occurs around these figures. No mint name is given on these or any other gold coin but this should not be taken to indicate that Edinburgh alone was responsible for striking this metal. It would appear that some heavy lions were struck at Perth and some light lions at Aberdeen and Dumbarton.

Robert III's lions seem to have been struck in some numbers and to have become an established feature of the currency. Sixty-three, along with sixty nobles of Edward III and seven of Richard II, were found hidden in Glasgow Cathedral. They do not appear to be worn and a

94 *Robert III, heavy lion, 1390-1403.*

95 *Robert III, heavy demi-lion.*

96 *Robert III, light lion, 1403-06.*

date of deposition for the hoard might be about 1400. An uncertain number of lions and groats, all of Robert III and seemingly of both his heavy and light coinages, were concealed on Balgony Farm, near Abernethy in Perthshire, probably during the first decade of the fifteenth century. A third discovery consisting of forty worn light lions of Robert was made at the church in Crieff, Perthshire, and may have been hidden later in the first quarter of the century. Single finds of gold coins are understandably rare but a lion of Robert has been found at Clifton, West Lothian, and a half noble of Edward III near North

Berwick. Despite the known finds being exclusively of Scottish and English coins, an Act of Parliament of 22 April 1392 allowed only lions and demi-lions, English and Flemish nobles and French crowns to have course throughout the kingdom. Some of the latter may have survived from the French subsidy of 50,000 gold francs sent in 1385.

Only pennies seem to have been struck during the early years of the reign of James I who succeeded in 1406. His release, from captivity in England, in 1424 meant the payment of another large ransom, of £40,000. He immediately set about administrative matters which included a major new coinage. A new gold coin emerged depicting the lion rampant within a lozenge (**97**). The reverse legend comes from the Psalms, 'Save thy people, O Lord', and the type consists of a saltire cross within a curved hexagram. In each curve is a quatrefoil and it is on the shape of this that the gold is classified. Group I possesses small quatrefoils with an annulet in the centre while on group II there are large open quatrefoils. Those on group III are similar but have a small pellet in the centre and on the more closed quatrefoils of group IV the central pellet is large. The gold, of which group II is the largest, corresponds to the fleur-de-lis groats and, like them, continued to be struck into the reign of James II until the latter's re-coinage of 1451. Groups I, II and III seem to be contemporary with the first and second varieties of the groats while group IV, with either annulet or saltire stops, corresponds with the third and fourth varieties of the groat assigned to James II.

97 *James I, demy, 1424-37, with large quatrefoils with open centres.*

This gold coin of James I and II is known as the demy. Since it is the main unit, the name is confusing but it refers to an attempted valuation at half an English noble. Only a small number of half demies, of group II alone, were struck. The demy was circulated at nine shillings and weighed 54 grains but suffered a reduction in fineness to 22 carats. The surviving moneyer's accounts of Robert Gray, for ten periods between

1434 and 1450, each refers to the striking of gold. Only work at the Edinburgh mint is recorded by Gray, but it seems likely that some demies were struck at Perth and Linlithgow. Some were certainly struck at Stirling, for in his account recorded in July 1443 the moneyer Alexander Tod records, 'auri...fabricati in dimidiis apud Strivelyng'. The gold was tested, satisfactorily, at a Trial of the Pyx in 1438.

There are few gold hoards of this period and the details of these are far from satisfactory. A mixed hoard of gold and silver found in a horn at Lochar Moss, Dumfriesshire, may have included demies along with English gold 'of the Henries'. Issues of Edward III and Robert III were also present in the discovery all of gold made at Dryburgh Abbey and perhaps hidden towards the middle of the century. The gold find from Cadder Castle, Lanarkshire, consisted of 118 coins of James I and II but exact issues and date of deposition are unclear. The finding of a single demy of James I is recorded from Hilton Farm, Perthshire.

While James I had to deal with the payment of his ransom, James II was more fortunate to be in receipt of a large dowry, of 60,000 gold crowns, on his marriage to Mary of Guelders in 1449. It is difficult to tell if this improvement in the royal finances was a factor in the subsequent coinage of 1451. However, that year saw the start of the first major re-coinage since 1424 and the introduction of the 'crown and pellets' groats. The regulations for the new coinage also ordered the striking of a gold lion with a return to the types used under Robert III, 'with the prent of a lyon on the ta side and the ymage of Sanct Andru on the tother side' (**98**). The first, and short-lived issue, continues the 'Save thy people, O Lord' legend of the demy but the second, and main issue, reverts to that of, 'Christ rules, Christ conquers, Christ commands'. A later group within the second issue has crowned lis instead of crowns only on either side of the obverse shield. The crown was to be of the same weight and fineness as the demy but its value was raised to ten shillings. It appears that Edinburgh was the only mint to produce the gold and the moneyer's accounts from 1464 to 1467

98 *James II, lion, 1451-60.*

show continued striking of the crown into the early years of the reign of James III and perhaps even into the 1470s.

James III commenced his own coinages about 1467 and innovation was the hallmark in all metals. Two gold coins were introduced, the rider and the unicorn. However, the rider does not appear to have been struck until about 1475, for it is not mentioned in the records before the account of the moneyers Alexander Livingstoun and Thomas Tod dated 27 July 1476. The obverse depicts the King, in armour, on horseback at full gallop while the reverse bears the lion rampant in a crowned shield with the 'Save thy people, O Lord' legend (**99**). A second issue, now accompanied by rare half and quarter riders, has the King riding to the left (**100-101**). These two issues of riders tie in with

99 *James III, rider, 1475-83, with rider to right.*

100 *James III, rider, 1475-83, with rider to left.*

101 *James III, half rider, 1475-83.*

the second and third mullet issues, groups III and IV, of James III's groats. The latter ceased in 1484. The rider was thus in production between 1475 and 1484 and seems to have been struck only at Edinburgh, though it is possible some were struck at Berwick when the town was in Scottish hands and active as a mint in the 1470s.

Although the earliest reference in the moneyers' accounts occurs in that for 1487, a legal document of 1485 makes mention of the second new gold coin. It was to remain in production until 1525 and was only ever struck at Edinburgh. The obverse depicts an unicorn supporting a shield with the lion rampant. On the reverse is a wavy star over a cross fleury. Oddly, in the first issue, both sides bear the same legend, EXUR-GAT DEUS ET DISSIPENTUR INIMICI EIUS ('Let God arise, and let His enemies be scattered'). Although later unicorns had a slightly lower fineness, those of the first issue appear to be 22.5 carats fine. It is thought to have been a small issue but in the inventory made after the King's death in 1488, his coffers were found to contain 180 riders, 980 unicorns, 1,000 crowns and 5,000 demies. Hoards and stray finds of such pieces continue to be virtually non-existent and it is only from the subsequent reign that they begin to be recorded again.

James IV's coinage began in 1489 with the gold continuing to be the unicorn, though its fineness was reduced to between 21 and 19 carats (**102**). The King's name and title appear on the obverse and a first issue is distinguished by the crown around the unicorn's neck having three lis. The later unicorns possess a crown with five lis and have Old English lettering and then the new Roman lettering. The date of the change is uncertain and it is unclear how late into the reign the unicorns were struck. Half unicorns were also struck (**103**). At some stage, possibly separating the two issues of unicorns, a small number of lions – by then called Scottish crowns – were also issued, mainly of the previous type, but first a version showing St. Andrew holding his cross. The unicorns were current for eighteen shillings and the lions for thirteen shillings and fourpence. Both emanated from Edinburgh alone and the records show the bullion to have included links taken from the King's gold chains and also French crowns. The Treasurer's account rendered in 1506 records that no less than 3,696 such pieces were re-struck as Scots coins, presumably unicorns. James's marriage in 1503 to Margaret Tudor brought the royal coffers a dowry of £10,000. Payments made by the King to foreigners seem mainly to have been in unicorns as a matter of prestige.

Towards the end of the century there appears to have been a sudden rise in the number of hoards containing gold. A single lion of James II was included with the 256 silver and 2 copper coins hidden at

102 James IV (1488-1513), unicorn, second type, with crown of five lis on unicorn.

103 James IV, half unicorn.

Innerwick, East Lothian, about 1488 and a little group of 2 unicorns of James III and IV along with an illegible silver coin was found in the ruins of a chapel near Luss, Argyllshire. There was also a James IV unicorn among 8 gold and 150 silver coins recovered at St Andrews. Gold accounted for 30 of the 32 coins found at Wick. Here the Scottish and English element was mainly of James I and II and Henry VI while the European coins consisted of a Burgundian rider and 5 French écus, suggesting concealment perhaps in the 1490s. This is one of the earliest records of foreign gold being found in a hoard despite its frequent mention in the written records.

A single Burgundian half noble of 1488 accompanied the seventeen riders and unicorns of James III and IV in the huge 1920 Perth hoard, mainly composed of silver and billon coins and hidden after 1496. A solitary lion of James II was found in a smaller hoard of 243 silver and billon coins recovered at Whitburn, Linlithgowshire, and also hidden after the new coinage of 1496. The date of deposition of a hoard found in Dumfries in 1615 is uncertain but the find is interesting in being the subject of one of the earliest cases of Treasure Trove recorded in Scotland. Some gold, and seemingly silver coins as well as a gold chain were found but 'most undewtiffullie conceallit' by one William

Turnour. He was committed to the Tolbooth in Edinburgh to await the pleasure of the law and among the eighteen gold coins confiscated were four unicorns and six French pieces. This is typical of the hoards centred on 1500, in which gold is present but not in large numbers and usually additional to the main contents of silver and billon. There seems to have been little English gold available and the more prominent Scottish issues, especially unicorns, are now accompanied by some continental gold.

The unicorn continued to be the gold coin in the early part of the reign of James V. The disaster of Flodden Field occurred in 1513 when James was only one year old and for the period of his minority until 1526 the country was ruled by a regent. The Privy Council discussed the coinage in 1515 and it would appear that sometime between then and 1517 there was a small issue of eagle crowns. The eagle, on the reverse, is in fact a dove representing the Holy Spirit and around it are the name and titles of John, Duke of Albany, the Regent. None is known to be extant. It was not until 1517 that the first mention of actual coins appears in the records. Two licences were given to coin eighty and thirty ounces of gold into unicorns. One of the licencees was James, Earl of Arran, who received further permission to have unicorns struck in 1518 and 1519. There was, however, a difficulty in 1518 for when the chest containing the dies was delivered to the Treasurer the keys could not be found and the locks had to be forced.

104 James V, first coinage, 1513-26, gold unicorn.

The types, weight and fineness of James V's unicorns remained unchanged and they were current at twenty shillings (**104**). They can be distinguished by the Roman lettering and the lack of a numeral after the King's name. Some have a reverse of James IV and on these there is also to be seen the first countermark, a cinquefoil, found in the Scottish series. The same cinquefoil is found on some reverses bearing a small mullet in the centre of the wavy star. Since the cinquefoil was an emblem of the the Earls of Arran, those bearing this device may be associated with the strikings of 1517-19. The main issue of unicorns appears to be of those with this mullet but without a countermark though sometimes a pellet replaces the mullet and sometimes nothing is found in the centre. A few half unicorns are known, of the main issue only.

The regency was ended in 1524 though the King's guardian, the Earl of Angus, Archibald Douglas, wielded the power until his downfall in 1528. Parliament set up a commission in 1524 to consider a new coinage, of which the gold was to be coined from native metal. The Privy Council, meeting early in 1526, ordered the new coinage to consist of a gold crown and a silver groat. The chest for the dies was to have two keys and samples of the coins were to be put aside for the Trial of the Pyx. James Achesoun, a burgess of the Canongate, was appointed Master Moneyer and his contract was approved by Parliament towards the end of the year.

105 James V, second coinage, 1526-38, gold crown.

The obverse of the crown bears the arms of Scotland with a saltire on either side and the numeral 5 after the King's name. A cross fleury with a thistle head in each angle constitutes the reverse type (**105**). The crowns are divided into four groups which correspond with those of the contemporary profile portrait groats. Again an early type, group I, has a transitional reverse legend, PER LIGNUM CRUCIS SALVI SUMUS – 'By the wood of the cross we are saved'. This is changed on group II to CRUCIS ARMA SEQUAMUR – 'Let us follow the arms of the cross'. Annulet stops are found on both, while groups III and IV possess trefoil and pellet stops respectively. Though weighing slightly less, they are of the same fineness and value, twenty shillings, as the earlier unicorns. James V's second issue gold coins were known as 'Abbey Crowns' which is the earliest indication that a mint had been opened at Holyrood where earlier in the century the new palace had been completed beside the twelfth-century abbey. It is uncertain if it struck any coins earlier than these but its location is known to have been in the outer courtyard of the palace, on the Canongate.

The second coinage continued until 1538 when it was replaced by a third and final issue consisting of gold and billon only. The crown was replaced by a new coin, called the ducat, current for forty shillings and weighing 88.34 grains of 23 carats fineness. The ducat is perhaps one of the most pleasing of Scottish coins with a fine portrait of the King wearing a bonnet – which gives the coins their alternative name of 'bonnet pieces'. It is a much better, and probably a more true, portrait than that found on the groats of 1526-38. The piece is also significant in bearing a date, 1539 (**106**) and then 1540, and of the two the latter seems to bear a more finely cut portrait (**107**). The reverse bears the arms of Scotland superimposed on a cross fleury with the legend, HONOR REGIS IUDICIUM DILIGIT ('The king's honour loves justice'). Two-thirds and one-third ducats, of 1540 only, were also struck (**108-109**).

106 James V, third coinage, 1538-42, gold ducat, 1539.

107 Ducat, 1540.

James Achesoun had refused to strike the new billon coins and was replaced as Master Moneyer by Alexander Orrok, of Sillebawby, though the work was carried out by Richard Wardlaw and Richard Young. They proved unable to complete the task and Achesoun was back in 1540 as Orrok's colleague. The more competent ducats with

108 Two-thirds ducat, 1540.

109 One-third ducat, 1540.

the date 1540 are therefore probably his work and ducats, as well as the fractions, were struck until 1542 albeit with the date unchanged. The Treasurer's account for the year to September 1541 records 130 ounces of gold, mined on Crawford Muir and Corehead, coined into ducats by Achesoun and again the account of August 1542 records ducats struck from 159 ounces of 'auri Scotiani'.

The major gold hoard recorded from James V's reign is that from Dunblane which ended with crowns of the second coinage which lasted to 1538. A total of 180 coins was found in a pottery jug of which about half were Scottish extending back to issues of James I. The thirteen English nobles and angels ran from Edward III to Henry VIII while the remaining eighty-five pieces were French écus apart from a single issue of Burgundy. A small hoard of about twenty coins found in the High Street in Perth seems to have been entirely foreign in content, again mainly French with three Spanish and one Portuguese piece. A large hoard of gold and silver from Eddleston, Peeblesshire, seems to be dated by an unspecified gold coin of James V and the find of gold coins of Henry VIII made in Haddington, East Lothian, may also have been hidden around this time. Although English gold coins still figured in the periodic lists of values fixed during the first half of the sixteenth century, it is mainly Scottish and French coins which made up the gold coin in circulation.

CHAPTER SIX
Billon and Copper

Debasement by means of increasing the amount of alloy was introduced by Robert III at the end of the fourteenth century. At first it affected the penny and halfpenny only, and later was generally confined to the minor denominations. Debased or billon pennies, and less so halfpennies, were to become an increasingly prominent feature of the coinage and currency as the fifteenth century progressed. Groats on the whole escaped this form of debasement but as their value rose the gap in the system between pennies and groats of twelve pence and more was filled by new billon coins, such as the plack of fourpence (or more likely sixpence) from the reign of James III and the bawbee of sixpence from the reign of James V. James III also issued a number of small copper coins but the experiment was not repeated and copper was not struck again until 1597.

The debased pennies and halfpennies of Robert III's heavy coinage are of the same types as his larger silver coins. The bust is now facing as in England and the legend abbreviated while the reverse has groups of three pellets instead of the previous mullets and the single legend only permitted by the smaller flan reads, VILLA EDINBURGH. The Act of 1393 ordered that pennies were to be struck of which four were to have as much silver as one groat but were to weigh proportionately as much as six pennies because of the added alloy. Halfpennies of the same metal and proportionate weight were also to be struck and together they were to make up a fifth of the proposed coinage. The weight of the penny should therefore be 17.25 grains and the fineness about .617 but they rarely reach this weight and many seem more base.

At first the bust is rather rough in style and the lettering large. Such pieces were struck only at Edinburgh. In both respects the second issue is of much neater appearance and now Perth, and later Aberdeen, join Edinburgh as mints. However, both issues are rare and no small denominations were coined during the new light coinage of the last years of the reign. A few single finds of Robert III pennies have been recorded from excavations at St. John's Tower, Ayr, Threave Castle and the Meal Vennel in Perth.

The only coins assigned to the first part of James I's reign are billon pennies and halfpennies. Apart from the change in name, these continue to depict a facing bust with a cross and pellets reverse and can be distinguished from the later issues by the absence of an initial mark before the reverse legend. A fairly large number of these class A coins seem to have been struck at Edinburgh with smaller amounts of pennies only at Aberdeen and Inverness. These last two mints may have been occasioned by the unsuccessful attempt of the Macdonalds of the Isles to expand across northern Scotland in 1411.

Immediately after his release James I instituted a major coinage, of which the fleur-de-lis groats are the main element. The four varieties of this groat were struck from 1424 until 1451, well into the reign of James II. The billon pennies of classes B and C belong to James I with some extension beyond the end of the reign in 1437. They now possess an initial mark of a cross before the VILLA which for class B is either Edinburgh or Inverness and for class C Edinburgh or Aberdeen. Halfpennies are known only for the former class of Edinburgh. The two classes correspond to the first and second varieties of the fleur-de-lis groats though the pennies do not have the sceptre introduced on the groats. The bust on some of the group C pennies is rather small and is clearly the result of the use of the halfpenny punch.

Group D pennies belong to James II and correspond to the third variety of fleur-de-lis groat which commenced sometime after 1437 and was replaced by the fourth variety towards 1451. No group D halfpennies are known and no small denominations at all seem to have accompanied the fourth variety groats. These final pennies seem to have been struck in small numbers and emanated from Edinburgh and Stirling. There are few records relating to the coinage from the reign of James I and only the moneyer's account for 1425 refers to the striking of 'minuta pecunia'. However, references to the coining of pennies and halfpennies occur in the accounts rendered in 1441-3. It is difficult to know to what extent the billon pennies circulated as hoards of any coins are rare from the first half of the fifteenth century but both pennies and halfpennies of James I have been found at Ayr, Inverkeithing and Linlithgow.

The main issue of billon of James II belongs to his re-coinage of 1451 named after the crown and pellets, groats. This is a short and small early issue on which the bust continues to be clothed as on the latest variety of fleur-de-lis groat. Besides the clothed bust, these pennies, of Edinburgh, have pellets in two quarters only. The other two quarters are plain. No halfpennies were struck now or during the course of the main second issue. However, there are a few transitional coins with a clothed bust and one angle of the cross with a crown and three with pellets and a central annulet. The same reverse is then found with the new unclothed bust which with a reverse of pellets in all four angles constitutes the type of the second issue pennies. Small numbers of these were struck at Aberdeen, Perth and Roxburgh but Edinburgh produced the majority.

The discovery, during excavation, of an important hoard of 358 coins at Leith in 1980 has enabled the second issue pennies to be classified more clearly. The hoard consisted of a small number of silver groats and halfgroats as well as 327 pennies of James II and III and may have been the 'till' money of a shopkeeper stolen and discarded on the refuse dump of Leith. Among the three types noted, type B is the largest and most diverse in terms of initial marks and privy marks. This is then subdivided by the obverse initial mark, crown, plain and lis. Aberdeen and Perth seem to have struck only fairly early in the issue and Roxburgh at the end, probably at the time of the successful siege of 1460. The weight of the pennies dropped after 1451 to around 10 grains and unlike the groats which appear to have been struck through to 1467, the striking of pennies may have ceased shortly after the death of James II in 1460. However, they were numerous enough to be still present in some numbers in the hoards found at Rhoneston and Glenluce hidden over thirty years later.

The billon of James III proves as complicated as his issues in the precious metals. It consists mainly of pennies struck solely at Edinburgh, and throughout with the basic types of a facing bust and cross and pellets reverse. It is divided into four classes A-D. The 106 class A specimens included in the Leith hoard have enabled these to be subdivided on the grounds of the initial mark on the reverse, whether or not there is an additional mark within the pellets: a crown initial mark occurs either with no mark or with points between the pellets, while a cross fourchée is found with either nothing, or points, saltires or annulets between the pellets. Many possess a B instead of a R in the inscription, a substitution which is a feature of English coins of 1470-71 but class A may date back to 1465 and it seems to have continued into the 1470s. A large amount of coin struck 'in minuta pecunia' is recorded in the account rendered by the moneyer Alexander Tod in 1464. The average weight appears to be around 7 grains.

Class B pennies are very rare and seem to have been struck in only small numbers. Not a single specimen occurred in the Leith hoard, only one in the Glenluce hoard and none in the Rhoneston find. They are easily recognizable in having a cross fourchée on the reverse and slipped trefoils or quatrefoils instead of pellets in the angles. The cross fourchée associates them with the first portrait groats (group II) which possess a similar cross. It is uncertain when they were struck, probably sometime during the 1470s.

James III's class C billon pennies are a numerous group, found in both the Glenluce and Rhoneston hoards, and are subdivided on the contents of the former into Ci -Cv. These can be distinguished by the shape of the bust and crown. The first three subgroups correspond to the group III mullet groats in production from about 1475 to 1482; Cii is the main issue. The later two subgroups Civ and v belong with the group IV mullet groats and like them were struck in the few years prior to the final large coinage of 1484. The bust is the same as that used on the group IV silver pennies then current for threepence. The group D billon pennies are a rare and small issue. They can be associated with the second portrait groats, group VI, of 1484-8.

The innovation among the billon coinage lies with the plack. However, it is not until 1473 that they are first mentioned and only in relation to the stopping of further production. In an Act of Parliament of July 1473 it was ordered, 'as tuiching the plakkis....the lordis thinkis that the striking of thame be cessit'. This may have been only a temporary measure and it seems likely that a large number of placks was struck throughout the 1470s. The obverse of the new coin has a tressure with a shield and lion rampant with a small cross above and on either side. The reverse bears a floriate cross fourchée with a crown in each angle and a saltire in the centre. The single reverse legend reads, VILLA EDINBURGH and this is the only mint for the piece, believed to have been valued initially at fourpence and of .500 fineness (110). Half placks were also struck (111). A later Act of 1485 called in 'all the new plakkis last cunyeit' and it thus appears that there was a further small issue about 1483 or 1484 just before the second portrait groat coinage began. It has been suggested that the rare placks with an I in the centre of the reverse instead of the saltire are to be identified with this issue.

110 James III, billon plack.

111 Similar, half plack.

However, the more enigmatic and novel of James III's coinages are those in copper. In the main these are described as farthings. Type I has a large crown only on the obverse with the King's name and title. The reverse possesses a saltire cross with a small saltire either side and the mint name of Edinburgh (112). Type II has a crown above the initials IR and a crown upon a saltire cross with small saltires in each angle. Its legends are as on the previous group (113). Type III's obverse again has a crown over IR but the reverse type changes to a long cross with crowns and mullets of six points in alternate angles. The reverse legend

112 James III, copper farthing, type I, with crown on obverse. [enlarged x2]

113 Similar, type II, with IR crowned on obverse and a crown over a saltire cross on the reverse. [enlarged x2]

114 Similar, type IV, with large trefoil on obverse and a cross with crowns and mullets on the reverse. [enlarged x2]

takes various abbreviated forms of MONETA PAUPERUM ('Money of the Poor'). Type IV was given a quite different obverse of a large trefoil with a lis in each of the internal angles and a crown in the outer ones and no legend at all. However, its reverse is similar to that on type III but the cross is a cross fourchée and the mullets, in each of the four angles, are mainly of five points (**114**).

In addition there is a larger copper coin to which the most satisfactory name so far applied is the 'crux pellit penny'. The obverse has an orb, tilted at various angles to give three subgroups, all with the legend, IACOBUS DEI GRA REX. The reverse depicts a cross within a double four-arc tressure and the legend, CRUX PELLIT OMNE CRIMEN ('The cross takes away all sin') (**115-117**). Despite various former attributions, it seems most likely that these copper issues should all be regarded as regal issues, of James III. However, there remains much uncertainty as regards the sequence and dates of issue of what was officially and commonly called 'black money'. An anchor-point does exist in the Coinage Act of October 1466 which ordered 'there to be cunyeit (coined) copper money four to the penny, having in prente on the ta part the crois of Saint Androu and the croune on the tother part, with

115 James III, copper crux pellit penny, type I.

116 Similar, type II.

117 Similar, type III.

the superscripcione of Edinburgh on the taparte and ane R with James on the tother parte'. Alas none of the farthings fits this description exactly but the copper farthings of 1466 are generally associated with those of type I. A year later an Act of 12 October 1467 ordered their striking 'to be cessyt' and that no more were to be struck. They continue to be referred to in the records and in the Act of 20 November 1469 the only black money to be accepted throughout Scotland was that of 'Oure Souerane lordis awne blac mone strikkin and prentit be his cunyouris'. It thus seems that further strikings did take place and these are thought to correspond with the type II farthings. They have been given a central date of about 1470 which would fit in with production in the late sixties and early seventies.

The records then become silent but a date in the 1470s for type III with the six-point mullets would tie in the the six-point mullet groats though these were in issue from about 1467. It is possible there was an overlap in issue in the same way that the first portrait groats were struck at the same time as some of the mullet groats. A second anchor-point is to found in the crying down of the unsatisfactory black money in 1482 following the hanging of some of the King's favourites, including Cochrane, at Lauder Bridge. The type IV farthings with the trefoil would therefore have to have been in circulation before then and a date of circa 1480 might be reasonable especially as the five-point mullet appeared on the groats about 1482.

This may be the same Cochrane who has been associated with the much denigrated 'Cochrane's placks' and it has been suggested that the 'threepenny penny' cried down after Lauder is Cochrane's plack and is further to be identified with the crux pellit penny. Previous ecclesiastical attribution of the crux pellit coins to a mint at Crossraguel Abbey and subsequently to Bishop Kennedy of St Andrews are no longer in favour and a regal issue seems preferable. However, recent research suggests that Cochrane was much less important than considered by earlier historians and there is no documentary evidence to connect him with the issue of coinage. The fact of calling them after Cochrane may be seen in the same way as the term 'Stirling turners' of the 1630s refers to that nobleman being assigned the profit on the copper coinage by Charles I. Again the term 'plack' may be taken in a general sense and not as specifically applied to the contemporary billon placks. If Cochrane's placks and the crux pellit pennies are one, a date of issue in the mid or late 1470s until 1482 seems likely. Evidence for the suggestion that the crux pellit pennies are of continental origin remains unsatisfactory, though continental derivatives are known.

When the black money was cried down in 1482, it was described as 'innumerabill of copper'. However, recorded finds were few until the discovery made in the drainage system at Crossraguel Abbey, Ayrshire, in 1909. This brought to light 51 of the pennies and 126 of all types of the farthings, of which 21 were of brass. Types III and IV with the cross and mullets reverse were the most common. The pennies have continued to turn up and now appear to be quite common finds. A single specimen survived in the Innerwick hoard of silver coins concealed about 1488. The farthings also are recovered much more frequently than before. Type I, often on a squarish flan, is more numerous than type II and mules of these two issues have been found at Perth and Linlithgow. Types III and IV seem to be less common but two were recovered at Ayr. The 1466 Act had ordered 3,000 pounds of the new farthings and gives a rare indication of the intentions behind such a coinage. They were to pass in payment for the daily staples, 'brede and Ale', and other goods but for larger payments could only be given for one shilling in the pound.

The experiment of a copper coinage was not to be repeated for over a century and the lower denominations struck by James IV are confined to billon placks and pennies. The placks are the main coinage of the reign and are very common (**118**). They differ from those of James III by having crowns, instead of crosses, on either side of the shield. Old

118 James IV, billon plack.

English lettering continued in use at first, occurring on varieties with and without QRA at the end of the obverse legend. Some mules of the latter with QRA and Roman letters are found before Roman lettering with the numeral 4 after the King's name becomes the norm. Unfortunately it is not certain when the style of lettering changed but it seems to have been late in the reign. Somewhat earlier the plack had become the main coin in production. Records for this reign's coinage are not helpful but the account of 1505 refers to the coining of placks and that of 1512 records the use of some silver bowls for such coins.

All the billon pennies of James IV were struck before the introduction of the Roman lettering. They are divided into a first and second issue associated with the heavy and light groats respectively, struck before and after 1496. The first issue has a tall bust with and without annulets by the neck. The second is recognizable by having crowns and lis in the angles of the reverse cross (**119**). An early subgroup of the first issue has SALVUM FAC POPULUM TUUM DOMINE ('Save thy people, O Lord') on the reverse instead of the mint name which, of Edinburgh only, re-appears on subgroups II to IV with a small, large and round bust respectively. The pennies of James IV are quite common. An important group of 25 of the first issue forms a main element in the Glenluce hoard while 36 of the 219 billon coins deposited at Creggan,

119 James IV, billon penny, second issue, with round bust (IV).

120 James V, first coinage, 1513-26, billon plack.

Argyllshire, after 1513 were second issue pence. Again on the west coast, at Barr in Ayrshire, a pirlie pig, or pottery money box, was hidden about 1513 with 578 billon pieces of which 488 were James IV pennies. They also occur commonly among archaeological finds and as stray finds.

It was to be forty years before billon pennies were struck again but meanwhile the plack continued to be one of the major pieces of the coinage. During the first coinage of James V struck from 1513 until 1526 only unicorns (and some eagle crowns) and placks were struck. The placks are similar to those of James IV with Roman lettering but no numeral is given after the King's name and two of the crowns on the reverse are replaced by saltires. The stops consist of stars, pellets and trefoils (**120**).

Virtually no billon was coined during the second coinage of 1526-38 and it was the proposal of 1538 to introduce a new billon coin which made James Achesoun step down from his office of Master Moneyer. The new coinage went ahead under his replacement Alexander Orrok of Sillebawby, who it would seem gave his name to the new coin. The obverse depicts a large crowned thistle head with I and 5 on either side. The reverse consists of a saltire cross with a lis either side and the legend, OPPIDUM EDINBURGI (**121**). Half and quarter bawbees were also

121 James V, third coinage, 1538-42, billon bawbee.

122 Similar, half bawbee.

123 Similar, bawbee with annulets.

struck (**122**). The use of an annulet privy mark over the I, the 5 or both is common (**123**). They were issued at a fineness of .250 and perhaps as many as a million and a half were struck between 1539 and the end of the reign in 1542. The moneyers under Orrok, Richard Wardlaw and Richard Young, proved unequal to the task and by 1540 Achesoun was back at the mint. The bawbee proved to be a very successful piece and its continuing production leads into the coinages of Mary Queen of Scots.

CHAPTER SEVEN
Mary Queen of Scots

The death-bed fear of James V that his dynasty would end with his infant daughter was to prove unfounded. Mary Queen of Scots held the throne for twenty-five years and her son James VI was to unite the thrones of Scotland and England. The Stewarts, amidst much controversy, were to last some time and throughout continued to issue extensive coinages.

The coinage of Mary falls neatly into three phases from her accession in 1542 until her marriage, the short period of her marriage from 1558 until 1560 to Francis, Dauphin and then King of France, and finally the years of her personal rule in Scotland from her return in 1561 until her abdication in 1567. The pre-marriage issues might be termed the regency coinage, struck first under the authority of the Earl of Arran, Regent from 1542, and then under his replacement, the Queen Mother, Mary of Guise, from 1554. The former may be termed the cinquefoil issue for, with one exception, all the coins bear the cinquefoil emblem of James, Earl of Arran, on whose coat of arms it is also to be found.

Bawbees probably began to be struck early in 1543 and are really a continuation of those struck for James V who died on 14 December 1542. They are similar but for the change in name and title, M and R on either side of the thistle and the cinquefoils instead of the lis on the reverse (124). This was an extensive issue with the records showing it to have gone on until at least 1549. Further strikings took place in

124 Billon bawbee, 1542-58, Edinburgh.

125 Similar, with fluted cross.

126 Similar, half bawbee.

1554 including one to provide funds for the mission of the Bishop of Ross to France in relation to the Queen's proposed marriage. It has been estimated that over 4 million bawbees were issued and they can be classified by the shape of the crown and the lettering. On later pieces REGINA is reduced to R and the saltire cross becomes fluted (**125**). The bawbee continued to be struck at .250 fine and remained current for sixpence. Half bawbees were also struck (**126**).

The majority of Mary's bawbees bear the Edinburgh mint signature. However, one small group was struck at Stirling with the legend, OPPIDUM STIRLINGI (**127**). This fits in with the early Edinburgh baw-

127 Bawbee, Stirling, 1544.

bees and appears to have been struck at Stirling during the period from June to November 1544 when the mint was moved there. The reason for this was the appearance of an English army under the Earl of Hertford in pursuit of Henry VIII's 'rough wooing' of the Scots. The Queen Mother had taken the infant Queen to the greater security of Stirling Castle and an attempt was made to deprive Arran of the regency. These bawbees lack the Arran cinquefoil and in place of the saltire cross have a large cross potent, which was a Guise emblem and which re-appears on the later coins of the Queen Mother's regency. However, by November 1544 power, and coining, had returned to Arran's control.

128 Gold crown, 1543.

Among the Hopetoun Papers is an important manuscript entitled, 'Anent Cunyie ane ample discourses', which describes many of Mary's coinages. After noting the bawbee it continues, 'There were likewise coined a piece of twenty shillings bearing on the one side a M and a R of 23 carats fine and some abbey crowns'. The abbey crowns in Mary's name differ from those of her father only in having cinquefoils instead of saltires on the obverse and are presumed to have been struck from the beginning of the reign, perhaps immediately with a value of twenty-two shillings (**128**). The other gold coin, of twenty shillings, with the M and R and a cinquefoil beneath bears the sole date 1543. The MR is found on the reverse along with the legend, ECCE ANCILLA DOMINI ('Behold the handmaiden of the Lord') (**129**).

The only other coins struck during the first decade of Mary's reign are pennies issued in 1547 (**130**). An Act of the Privy Council of May that year refers to the great hurt and damage caused to the poor by the virtual disappearance of pennies and halfpennies and orders twelve stone to be coined. No halfpennies are known but pennies with an infantile bust and a cross with crowns and cinquefoils in the angles

129 *Gold twenty shilling piece, 1543.*

130 *Billon penny, with infant head, 1547.*

seems to fit this Act. The name of Edinburgh occurs on the reverse, and differences in the appearance of the bust suggest some numbers were struck, perhaps beyond 1547.

There were no further issues until 1553. A gold coinage consists of forty-four shilling pieces with the royal arms on the obverse and a complicated monogram of MARIA REGINA on the reverse with the legend, DILIGITE IUSTICIAM ('Observe Justice') (**131**). Rare specimens bear on both sides the initials IG for IACOBUS GUBERNATOR, the Regent James,

131 *Gold forty-four shilling piece, 1553.*

132 Similar, twenty-two shilling piece.

Earl of Arran, or possess instead cinquefoils on both sides but the more common variety has IG on the obverse and cinquefoils on the reverse. Twenty-two shilling pieces of this last variety only were also struck (**132**). All bear the date 1553.

133 Silver portrait testoon (group I), 1553.

In the same year a silver coinage commenced in the form of a new denomination called the testoon, worth four shillings. It bears a portrait of Mary, then approaching her eleventh birthday. The worn condition of most surviving specimens fail to do it justice. The reverse has the royal arms with a cinquefoil either side and the legend, DA PACEM DOMINE ('Give peace, O Lord') and the date 1553 (**133**). It appears that the dies were made and displayed at the new Paris mint by James Achesoun in October and that he then brought them across to Edinburgh for use. The appearance of these gold and silver coins may have been connected with the setting up of an establishment in France for Mary that same year.

The Hopetoun manuscript further notes, 'upon 18th November 1554 the Earl of Arran being governor demitted his authority to queen Mary, mother and regent to the queen's majesty'. Mary of Guise was to hold the regency until her death in 1560. Her first recorded act in relation to the coinage was to grant a licence to the French ambassador to have struck an issue of pennies similar to those of 1547 but with lis in two of the angles on the reverse instead of Arran's cinquefoil. However, it was not until 1555 that any major change took place. Then a new office of General of the Mint was instituted with David Forres as the first holder. The post of Master continued, with an Englishman, John Misserwie, recorded in 1555 but replaced later that year by John Achesoun. There were now to be two Wardens, both more closely concerned with production than in the past. The accounts of the Lord High Treasurer for 1564 show that the General was in receipt of a monthly salary of twelve pounds and ten shillings. The same accounts for January 1561 record payment for the building of a mint at Edinburgh Castle and repair of the mint at Holyrood Palace during 1560. This would suggest that the bulk of Mary's coinage at least up to 1560 was struck at Holyrood.

134 *Gold three pound piece, 1555.*

135 *Similar, thirty shilling piece.*

Gold and silver were both issued in 1555 by the Master, John Misserwie. Gold three pound and thirty shilling pieces bear a rather disappointing portrait of Mary (**134-135**). The royal arms are found on the reverse with the legend, IUSTUS FIDE VIVIT ('The just man lives by faith'). The most common date is 1555 thought the date may have remained unchanged during strikings in 1556 for that date does not occur. Further pieces bear the dates 1557 and 1558 but these are rare and presumably not produced in large numbers.

136 Testoon (group II), 1555.

The testoon of 1555 has a simple crowned M with a thistle head either side on the obverse (**136**). Its reverse type is the lion rampant within a shield upon a cross potent, an emblem associated with the Queen Mother's family of Guise and used on the Stirling bawbees eleven years earlier. The legend translates, 'The Lord loves a humble-heart'. It was struck in .725 fine silver and was current for five shillings. A new type appeared in 1556, of lower weight but in better silver, .916 fine, and with the same value. Such testoons, dated 1556 and 1557, possess the arms on the obverse with M and R either side and a large cross potent with a plain cross in each angle on the reverse. A variety, with the dates 1557 and 1558 (**137**), possesses a

137 Testoon (group III), 1558.

low-arched crown above the arms instead of the normal high-arched one. Both varieties are found with and without a small annulet privy mark under the M and R. The most common testoons are those of 1556 and 1557.

138 *Billon lion or hardhead, 1555.*

The simple crowned M design of the 1555 testoon was also used for a new denomination of one and a half pence called the lion. Its reverse type consists of a lion rampant with the legend, VICIT VERITAS ('Truth has conquered') (**138**). The official reason given for its striking was to assist with the daily purchase of 'vitallis sik as breid, drink, flesche, fische'. The earliest lions are dated 1555 and 1556 while a second issue took place in 1558, though the silver content of the latter was reduced to only one twenty-fourth.

139 *Billon 'vicit veritas' penny, 1556.*

Pennies were again struck in 1556 using the cross potent reverse type of the 1556-8 testoons on the obverse and with the simple reverse of a small crown above VICIT VERITAS 1556 in three lines (**139**). The plack made a brief comeback the following year. It is basically similar to that produced over thirty years earlier by James V. However, the mint name on the reverse is replaced by the legend, SERVIO ET USU TEROR ('I serve and am worn by use'). Often known as 'servio placks', they are dated 1557 (**140**).

140 Billon 'servio' plack, 1557.

In April 1558 Mary entered into marriage with Francis, the Dauphin, and into a new, though brief, period of her life. Within the space of three years she was successively Dauphiness, Queen and Dowager of France. In January 1558/9 the Privy Council ordered the striking of a new gold coin 'to be callit the king and quenis ducatt'. Francis and Mary face each other in the manner found on the English shillings and sixpences issued between 1554 and 1557 for Mary Tudor and Philip of Spain though the portraits on the latter are more successful. The inscription styles Francis and Mary as 'King and Queen of Scots and Dauphin and Dauphiness of Vienne'. The reverse has an attractive and novel cross composed of arms each of a pair of intertwined dolphins, an emblem of the dauphin, and with a cross of Lorraine in each angle. The ducats were struck by John Hairt, who temporarily replaced John Achesoun as Master, and made 'for the most from gold gotten from gilt chalices and other jewels'. It was probably a small issue for less then half a dozen are known to be extant.

The silver, in the form of testoons and halves, was more numerous with over a thousand stone weight being minted. The first were struck under John Achesoun from the beginning of December 1558 and bear the dates 1558 and 1559 (**141**). Like the ducats they give Francis the title 'King of Scots' which had not been ratified by the Scottish Parliament until the end of November. The obverse bears a shield with the arms of the Dauphin impaling those of Scotland, superimposed on a cross potent. On the reverse is a crowned FM monogram with a cross of Lorraine either side, giving rise to the term 'Lorraines'. The legend reads, FECIT UTRAQUE UNUM ('He has made the two, one'). The inscription is appropriate but the overall design is rather unsatisfactory.

In 1560 it was replaced. Indeed this was a period of change. Henri II died suddenly in July 1559 whereupon Francis and Mary found themselves King and Queen of France as well as of Scotland. Sometime in 1560 John Hairt replaced John Achesoun as Master of the Mint. In

141 *Silver testoon, 1559.*

June the Regent Queen Mother, Mary of Guise, died and the same year the reformed religion triumphed in Scotland. The new testoons would seem to reflect all these events. They appear to be the work of Hairt. The royal arms, now France impaling Scotland, accompany the double royal titles on the obverse. The FM monogram remains on the reverse but with a crowned lis and thistle either side (**142**). Gone are the emblems of the regency of Mary of Guise and it has been suggested that the inscription refers to the ascendency of the reformers, VICIT LEO DE TRIBU IUDA ('The lion of the tribe of Juda has prevailed'). Two varieties of the 'vicit leo' testoon, with high-arched or low-arched crown, are dated 1560 but those of 1561 are of the latter variety only. Half testoons, with both crowns, were struck in 1560 (**143**).

142 *'Vicit leo' testoon, 1560.*

Billon was also struck in considerable quantity during the period of Mary's marriage. An Act of the Privy Council of March 1558 ordered the issue of a new twelve penny groat at .500 fine. It was to have the crowned FM mongram with a dolphin either side on the obverse and an

143 Similar, half testoon.

inscription in four lines within a square on the reverse. This inscription, IAM / SUNT DUO / SED UNO / CARO ('They are no longer two, but one flesh') gives the coin its more popular name of the 'nonsunt' (**144**). Striking must have begun at once for the date, 1558, placed under the inscription, is found as well as 1559. There was also an issue of lions or hardheads with a similar obverse but the lion rampant on the reverse as on previous lions (**145**). Genuine pieces occur only with the dates 1559 and 1560. None of the billon bears the royal titles of France, so the previous Dauphin title continued in use even after July 1559. However, it is unlikely that any billon was coined after the death

144 Billon nonsunt, 1559.

145 Billon lion or hardhead, 1559.

of Mary of Guise in the summer of 1560. One of John Knox's strident criticisms concerned the 'corrupted scruiff and baggage of hardheads and nonsunts'.

146 *Mary, first widowhood, portrait testoon, 1561.*

147 *Similar, half testoon.*

Francis died in December 1560 and despite events in Scotland, Mary decided to return home. She disembarked at Leith in August 1561 and so began, when she was nineteen, the period of Mary's personal rule. Coinage was not neglected. John Achesoun had regained the mastership of the mint and he was to have charge of the production of a silver coinage of a testoon and its half though the punches and dies were the work of Antoine Brucher at the Paris mint. The obverses have what is probably Mary's best numismatic portrait while the reverse still depicts the arms of France impaling Scotland (**146-147**). The Salvum Fac legend makes a re-appearance and the date is found on a tablet beneath the Queen's head. Only the dates 1561 and 1562 occur and the issue appears to be small. It seems that a gold crown was comtemplated but neither gold nor billon was struck during the remainder of the reign.

No further coin was struck until after Mary's marriage to Henry, Lord Darnley, in 1565. By this time a larger crown- or dollar-sized silver coin had become common in Europe and the coinage ordered by the Privy Council in December 1565 was to consist of such a piece, to be 'callit the Marie ryall' and current for thirty shillings with two-thirds and one-third ryals also (**148-150**). The obverse depicts a crowned shield with the lion rampant and the legend is 'Mary and Henry Queen and King of Scots'. The reverse design consists of a tortoise climbing up a palm tree on which is a scroll with, DAT GLORIA VIRES ('Glory gives strength') and the date beneath. The legend sees a return of DEUS EXURGAT etc. Ryals were struck, still by John Achesoun, in 1565, 1566 and 1567 and the major source of the bullion appears to have been the previous silver coins. The fractions are confined mainly to 1565 and 1566. An experimental ryal, with Mary and Henry facing each other and with Henry's name first in the legend, seems to have circulated for a short time before the main issue. It is now very rare.

148 *Mary and Henry, silver ryal, 1565.*

149 *Similar, two-thirds ryal.*

150 Similar, one-third ryal.

Henry's murder in 1567 left Mary a widow for the second time though her widowhood was of short duration for she soon married the Earl of Bothwell. In the short intervening period further ryals and fractions dated 1567, and bearing Mary's name alone, were struck (**151-152**). The new marriage is not referred to on any coin and indeed soon led to Mary's abdication and flight.

151 Mary, second widowhood, ryal, 1567.

152 Similar, one-third ryal.

Over this period of twenty-five years it was billon which was produced in the greatest numbers though a substantial quantity of silver was also coined. Much of the latter, however, seems to have found its way out of the country. The small amount of Scottish gold was supplemented by foreign pieces particularly French and Portuguese. Much forged billon was imported and there were frequent Acts against its use. Action was taken, for in the Lord High Treasurer's accounts for 1566-7 there is reference to the execution of a burgess of Perth and the arrest of six merchants in Aberdeen for the same crime of importing false hardheads and placks from Flanders. It is perhaps in this respect that we should view the large hoard of several thousand false hardheads of Francis and Mary found in three bags near Marischal College in Aberdeen in 1847. Expediency may have dictated their concealment and arrest prevented their recovery.

Apart from this find, over thirty hoards are recorded from Mary's reign. Billon coins predominate among the contents though only a few small finds consist of billon alone. Most also include some silver and gold such as the 1963 find from Righead, Dumfriesshire, used to reclassify the bawbees of James V and Mary. The Righead jug contained 344 bawbees, 7 halves, 24 placks, 142 silver coins – mainly of Henry VIII – and 10 gold pieces of which 9 were French. Discoveries at Hawick and Abernethy, Perth, both contained over 500 coins though the precious metal content was much smaller and only of silver in the case of Abernethy. The latter ended with nonsunts, the former with hardheads, of Mary. Few other billon hoards exceed 100 coins. Bawbees, hardheads and nonsunts are most common with few servio placks and rarely pennies.

Silver was not perhaps as rare as sometimes appears. Half a dozen smallish hoards are of silver only and it is found as a small proportion of a further ten, mainly billon hoards. Much of this is Henry VIII's fine pre-1544 issues and only rarely is his base silver found. Indeed, in an unusual turnabout, the Scottish Privy Council in July 1545 banned the new debased English groat. Scottish silver, when it is included, is of the 1555-7 issue though some of Francis and Mary also occurs at which stage that of Henry VIII seems to have disappeared. Only two hoards, both from Glasgow, are of gold on its own. One contained over 800 pieces, the other 18 or 19 but both show the great variety of gold coins circulating in the country – Scottish, English and European, especially French. The small number of gold coins included in four of the billon hoards displays a similar picture.

Site and stray finds of Mary's coins are, not surprisingly, numerous. Most consist of hardheads of Mary or Francis and Mary as well as the 1557 servio placks but bawbees and pennies are rare and single finds of silver and gold very rare. If such a piece was dropped it was probably thoroughly searched for and returned to its place in the contemporary currency.

CHAPTER EIGHT
James VI and I

James VI was one year old when he succeeded his mother upon her abdication in 1567. Despite this, coins were issued at once in his name. A great many coinages and a great variety of coins were to be struck throughout the period from 1567 until 1603 when he also acquired the English throne on the death of Elizabeth I. However, the extensive use of dates on the coins and a greater number of surviving documents relating to the coinage make James's issues relatively straightforward. After 1603 the Scottish coinage changes to the English pattern and for over two decades until the end of the reign in 1625 there is little novelty.

153 *Silver ryal or 'sword dollar', 1570.*   **154** *Similar, two-thirds ryal, 1569.*

The first coinage was ordered in July 1567 and was to consist of the 'James ryall' of thirty shillings along with its two fractions (**153-154**). It was essentially a continuation of the last issue of Mary, and likewise no gold or billon was struck. However, the reverse type changed dramatically to a simple upright sword with the date on either side and a hand pointing to the value – XXX, XX and X (shillings) respectively. The legend reads, PRO ME SI MEREOR IN ME ('For me, or if I deserve, against me'). All three denominations were struck each year until

155 Silver half merk or noble, 1573.   *156 Similar, quarter merk 1572.*

1571. They were then replaced with a half and quarter merk in the next year. The value is given on the obverse and on the reverse is an ornate cross with crowns and thistle heads in the angles (**155-156**).

The new coins were struck at Dalkeith whither the mint had been moved for safety. Supporters of Mary were still occupying Edinburgh Castle and in 1572 are said to have copied the half and quarter merks, and coins of Mary's reign. However, the references are unclear and it has proved difficult to identify the so-called Marian issues from genuine pieces. Rare half and quarter merks with pellets in the arms of the cross may represent the earliest official strikings as well as the copies while those with bars may belong after the capture of the castle by the King's supporters in May 1573. The Marian moneyers, two Edinburgh goldsmiths, were executed and the mint returned to Holyrood.

However, the real problem as regards forgery continued to lie with the large amounts of forged placks and lions or hardheads manufactured abroad. An attempt was made to solve the problem in 1575 when all such coins were ordered to be bought into the mint so that those pieces found to be 'lawful and true coin of this realm' could be countermarked with a heart and star for return to circulation (**157**). Meanwhile the

157 Countermarking of 1575 – heart and star, on Mary 'servio' plack, 1557.

158 Gold twenty pound piece, 1575.

half merks and quarter merks were struck throughout the decade, bearing the dates 1572-7 and 1580. During this period James's first gold coin was issued. It is a magnificent piece weighing an ounce and valued at twenty pounds. The young King is depicted half-length in armour with a sword in one hand and an olive branch in the other, representing war and peace. A panel below contains the words, IN UTRUNQUE PARATUS ('Prepared for either'). The royal arms on the reverse are accompanied by the classical legend, PARCERE SUBIECTUS ET DEBELLARE SUPERBOS ('To spare the humbled and subdue the proud') (**158**).

The year 1578 witnessed another countermarking, though on this occasion one of revaluation. The price of silver had risen steeply with the result that the silver coins were suddenly worth more than their face value and were in danger of being melted down or exported as bullion. Consequently they were called in and struck with a simple crowned thistle countermark raising their value (**159**). In the case of the ryal or thirty shilling piece this now had a value of thirty-six shillings and ninepence. Testoons and halves of Mary as well as her ryals and fractions and those of James VI are found with this countermark. The half merks and quarter merks, which had been struck in silver only around .666 fine, were not included. The final striking of these took place in 1580, by which time they had been joined by a better quality silver coin of of .916 fineness. This two merk piece, or 'thistle dollar' after the finely executed thistle on the reverse, was coined in 1578, 1579 and 1580 (**160**). There is also a merk of the same type. These, together with the gold twenty pound piece and the debased half and quarter merks, make up James VI's second coinage.

159 Countermarking of 1578 – crowned thistle, on Francis and Mary testoon, 1558.

160 Silver two merk or thistle dollar, 1579.

It was followed by a small third coinage of gold and silver in 1580-81. An Act of the Privy Council ordered the striking of a gold piece to be called the 'Scottish ducat' of four pounds. Ducats dated 1580 depict a very young looking James wearing a high ruff (**161**). The silver, dated 1581 only, consists of a sixteen shilling piece along with smaller coins

161 Gold ducat, 1580.

of eight, four and two shillings. The sixteen shillings is essentially similar to the merk of 1579 and 1580, of thirteen shillings and fourpence, but again rising bullion prices had forced up the face value. The obverse coat of arms on the new coin is better executed but the thistle on the reverse is small and rather overshadowed by the crown now placed on top. Both coinages bear the new, and popular, legend, NEMO ME IMPUNE LACESSET ('No one shall hurt me with impunity')

No sooner were these in circulation than the Privy Council, in March 1581/2, ordered them to be 'brocht in agane to be cunyeit of new'. Preparations had begun earlier. In a rare insight into the design process of the coinage the Lord Treasurer's accounts record the payment in January of ten pounds to Lord Seton's painter for pictures of the King given to the die sinker to engrave the portrait for the new coinage. The dies were quickly produced for in February a payment of £100 was made to Thomas Foulis, a goldsmith, for this work. About the same time John Achesoun's long association with the mint ended and he was replaced as Master by his son, Thomas Achesoun. Sir Archibald Napier, appointed in 1576, continued as General of the Mint. The mint officials were ordered by the Privy Council to produce the new coinage in the house of one Archibald Stewart, for the mint at Holyrood, despite repairs recorded over the years, was ruinous and unfit for the task. This building, situated in the Cowgate, was to remain the home of the mint. Only briefly during the plague of 1585 was it ordered to be moved to Dundee, and then Perth, but if any coins were struck at either place they are not now recognized.

162 Silver thirty shilling piece, 1582.

The original Act ordered only silver ten shilling pieces with the King half-length in armour and holding a sword. On either side of the arms on the reverse are the initials I and R and below the value X and S. The legend, ending with the date, is, HONOR REGIS IUDICUM DILIGIT ('The king's honour loves justice'). The ten shilling piece was struck in 1582, 83 and 84. However, supply seems to have fallen short of demand for in April 1582 the Privy Council extended the range of values to forty, thirty (162) and twenty shilling pieces of the same design and with the forty shilling piece weighing one ounce. The latter is found only with the date 1582 and its excessive rarity suggests a low output. The others seem to have been struck mainly up to 1584 with a much smaller mintage in 1585 and 86, the time of the plague.

The silver was accompanied by an issue of gold which was ordered in 1584 and ceased in 1588. It is highly unusual in not having the King's name and title in the normal manner on the obverse. The obverse type, of a lion sejant holding an upright sword and sceptre in outstretched arms, possesses the legend, POST 5 ET 100 PROAVOS INVICTA MANENT HAEC ('After 105 ancestors these remain unconquered') (163). The reverse too is novel with a saltire cross whose arms are composed of a crowned IR, all four enclosing an S in the centre. This lion noble of seventy-five shillings was struck each year except for 1587. Smaller numbers of two-thirds (164) and one-third nobles were also struck.

163 Gold lion noble, 1585.   *164 Similar, two-thirds lion noble.*

The gold and silver of the fourth coinage was complemented by James VI's first coinage in billon ordered on Christmas Day 1583. No billon had been struck since 1560 and time, melting-down and forgery had taken their toll on this important feature of the coinage. The new billon, eightpenny and fourpenny groats or placks, were to be .250 fine. The obverse depicts the crowned arms and the reverse a crowned thistle with the mint name of Edinburgh around (165-166). Production, probably interrupted by the plague in 1585, seems to have continued until the beginning of August 1587 when the mint was ordered to cease

165 *Billon eightpenny plack, 1583-90.* **166** *Similar, half plack.*

striking billon. This order was proclaimed by a messenger and trumpeter at the mercat crosses in Edinburgh and other towns, for which service the Lord Treasurer made a payment of twenty shillings. However, an expedition against unrest in the north required financing and in July 1588 a further £11,500 was ordered for 'buying powder, bullets, victuals and all other provisions and preparations required for the furtherance of this action'.

A fifth coinage followed soon after. This consisted of a new billon twopenny plack with a reduced silver content of only one twenty-fourth as with the old lions or hardheads of 1558-60. When first ordered in August 1588, they were to have a crowned IR on the obverse and a lion rampant within a shield on the reverse and the legend, VINCIT VERITAS ('Truth conquers') (**167**). However, a change was made in November 1588 dispensing with the shield around the lion and adding two pellets, of value, behind the tail (**168**). The latter survive in large numbers and were accompanied by a rare penny plack with a single pellet of value (**169**).

This billon was accompanied by the issue of a gold coin based on the contemporary English rose noble. It was ordered by the Privy Council in September 1588 and was to have

167 *Hardhead or twopenny plack, August 1588.*   **168** *Similar, November 1588.*

169 Similar, half hardhead or penny.

'ane ship with his maiesteis arms and under the same ane thissil' (**170**). In the centre of the reverse was to be a thistle superimposed on a pair of crossed sceptres at each end of which was a small crown. These crowns alternate with lions in the internal angles of the tressure while in each of the outside angles is a small thistle head. A rather long legend translates, 'Sceptres flourish with the pious, God gives them kingdoms and unites them'. Though undated, they were probably struck over the next couple of years after 1588 since orders for two strikings are known for 1590. However, they are now rare and the proposed half thistle noble does not appear to have been produced.

According to an Act of Parliament of August 1591 there was now such a variety of coins in circulation that, with the exception of the thistle nobles and twopenny and penny placks, all were to be re-coined into new gold and silver pieces – James's sixth coinage. The Act does not specify the designs of these but again they diverge from past types. The single denomination in gold, of eighty shillings, depicts an older James wearing a tall hat, 'according to the painter's draft', from which they took the popular name of 'hat pieces'. The reverse is perhaps

170 Gold thistle noble, 1588.

171 Gold hat piece, 1592.

rather empty with a seated lion on the right side beneath a cloud, above which is the word 'Jehovah' in Hebrew. The legend, TE SOLUM VEREOR ('You alone do I fear') is found with the dates 1591, 92 or 93 (**171**).

The obverse type on the silver is the crowned arms, with a thistle on either side on the half merk of six shillings and eightpence, without the thistles on the quarter merk. The reverse, simple but symbolic, depicts a balance and upright sword with the legend, HIS DIFFERT REGE TYRAN-NUS ('In these a tyrant differs from a king') (**172**). This balance half merk was also struck from 1591 to 1593 but the quarter appeared only in 1591.

The hat pieces and balance half merks were thus of short duration and were replaced by the more substantial seventh coinage which, again it was said, was intended to replace the great and confusing diversity of coin in circulation. Gold, silver and billon were issued though this was to be the last time the latter specie was to be produced. Copper

172 Silver balance half merk, 1592.

replaced it in 1597. It was the billon which was ordered first, by an Act of Parliament dated 27 December 1593. This was to consist of a fourpenny plack, still only one twenty-fourth part silver, with a thistle upon a pair of crossed sceptres on the obverse and a small central lozenge with a thistle head on each point as the reverse type. The reverse retains the mint name, OPPIDUM EDINBURGI (**173**). The relief is somewhat low and these saltire placks, which are very rare, are usually in poor condition.

173 Billon saltire plack, 1594.

The gold and silver was ordered less than a month later. The gold five pound piece or rider takes its name from the fine equestrian portrait of the King which has the date, 1593-1601, below (**174**). The legend around the crowned arms on the reverse reads, SPERO MELIORA ('I hope for better things'). Half riders were also produced, though in small numbers, in some years. The portrait on the silver shows James bareheaded and in armour and is accompanied by a well-balanced triple-headed thistle on the reverse with the NEMO ME IMPUNE LACESSET legend. There are four denominations, ten and five shilling pieces as well

174 Gold rider, 1594.

175 *Silver ten shilling piece, 1593.*   **176** *Silver five shilling piece, 1595.*

as thirty and twelve pence pieces, with most dates from 1594 to 1601 for most of these values with the notable exception of 1596 and 7 for the two larger pieces (**175-176**).

The other notable feature of the seventh coinage is the re-introduction of copper, last produced in the fifteenth century. An Act of Parliament of May 1597 ordered the issue of copper twopences and pennies. They bear a similar portrait to that used on the the silver but on the reverse have three thistle heads and the mint signature (**177**). The penny, however, possesses a single pellet behind the King's head. The twopence clearly copies the French double tournois which has three lis on the reverse and it is presumably after the French coin that they were given the name 'turner'. The blanks were now prepared with machinery and though they were still then hammered by hand, the coins are well produced and an improvement on the earlier billon pieces.

177 *Copper turner or twopence, 1597.*

In 1601 the eighth and final coinage of James VI as King of Scotland alone was instituted. This is of gold and silver. The gold six and three pound pieces have the crowned arms on the obverse. The reverse type

178 Gold sword and sceptre piece, 1602.

179 Half sword and sceptre piece, 1601.

consists of a sword and sceptre crossed, with a crown above, a thistle head either side and the date below. The dates run from 1601 to 1604 and the legend is, SALUS POPULI SUPREMA LEX ('The safety of the people is the supreme law') (**178-179**).

These 'sword and sceptre pieces' were accompanied by silver with the same obverse design but with a return to a large single thistle on the reverse, lending the name 'thistle merk' to the largest piece. The legend reads, REGEM IOVA PROTEGIT ('God protects the king') with the date, 1601-4, after. The denominations consist of the merk (**180**), half, quarter and eighth merk or twenty pence.

180 Silver thistle merk, 1602.

James's coinages up to this time are diverse with a multitude of well thought out and executed types and inscriptions, of which the more unusual ones carry quite deliberate political propaganda. Although economic forces played some part in the continual re-coining, the profit motive was much to the fore and the income accruing to the King from his seignorage on the coinage was an important part of the royal income. James, however, was at considerable pains to emphasize that the re-coining was for the public good and that he was greatly concerned for the needs of the poor but perhaps he protested too much, too often. Nevertheless it resulted in a lively and fascinating series of coins between 1567 and 1603. This then ceased abruptly. Following the death of Elizabeth I, James succeeded her peacefully as the First of England. Although it was merely a union of the two crowns and each country remained independent, there was a drawing together of the coinages towards the less exciting English types.

Thus a uniform coinage emerged with only small differences between the Scottish coinage, minted at Edinburgh, and its English counterpart, struck at the Royal Mint on Tower Hill in London. The main difference lay in the use of the respective Scottish and English crowns, the former with a central lis and a cross on either side, the latter with a central cross and a lis on either side. The thistle was also used consistently as the Scottish initial mark and as the emblem on the two large silver coins whereas the English initial mark changed from year to year and the emblem was the rose. Otherwise the coins are of similar type, weight and fineness. The face value of the two coinages, however, had continued to draw further apart throughout the sixteenth century and by the start of the joint reign stood at a ratio of 12:1. Thus the largest piece, the gold unit, passed for twelve pounds Scots but one pound sterling while the smallest silver piece was worth twelve pence Scots and one penny sterling. Therefore the XII and the VI behind the King's head on the two main silver coins indicate shillings Scots but pence sterling. Nevertheless, for the first time since 1367, the coinages were freely interchangeable.

Production of the new coinage, James VI's ninth Scottish coinage, commenced in Edinburgh early in 1605. The obverse legends proclaim James, by the grace of God, King of Great Britain, France and Ireland. The gold unit bears a half length portrait of James crowned and holding a sword and orb. The gold double crown (six pounds Scots), Britain crown (three pounds Scots) and half-crown (thirty shillings Scots) depict a crowned bust. The reverses bear the crowned arms 'in ane new forme of shield quarterlie' with the English arms in the first and third quarters, the lion rampant in the second and the Irish harp in the fourth. The inscriptions make reference to the union of the crowns, respectively translating, 'I will make them one nation' on the unit, 'Henry (united) the roses, James the kingdoms' on the double and Britain crowns, and 'May God guard these united kingdoms' on the half-crown and thistle crown. The latter, worth four pounds Scots, completed the gold issue. It has a crowned rose on the obverse and a crowned thistle on the reverse.

181 Silver sixty shilling piece, 1604-09.

There are six silver denominations. The sixty shillings piece is the successor of the old ryal and the equal of the English crown (**181**). Both it and the thirty shilling piece have an equestrian portrait of the King with a thistle on the horse's cloth. The new arms, uncrowned, are found on the reverses. A bust is used on the twelve and six shilling pieces with XII and VI respectively behind. Again the arms are used on the reverses but on the six shilling piece the date appears above, examples with 1605, 6 and 9 (with the 9 punched over the 7) being known. On these four values the reverse legend is, QUAE DEUS CONIUNXIT NEMO SEPARET ('What God has joined together let no man put asunder'). In addition there are a two shilling and one shilling piece, both with a rose and thistle, the latter crowned only on the larger coin.

In 1609 it was ordained that the arms on the Scottish coins should be changed to the form as on the great seal of Scotland, that is to say with the lion rampant in the first and third quarters (**182-183**). Otherwise the values and types of the tenth coinage are unchanged. The six shilling pieces bear the dates of each year from 1610 until 1619 as well as 1622. Meanwhile a shortage of small change led to a second issue of copper turners in 1614. The types are now a triple-headed thistle and a lion rampant with two pellets behind (**184**). The King's titles are given in full form running from the obverse on to the reverse. Another issue of copper took place in 1623 but with the titles in an abbreviated form (**185**). Pennies of the same types were struck on both occasions (**186**).

182 *Gold double crown, 1609-25.*

183 *Silver twelve shilling piece, 1609-25.*

Despite such a long reign, spanning almost sixty years, the number of hoards to have survived drops considerably. Less than twenty are known from the first part of the reign up to 1603, and of these only fifteen are well enough recorded to give some indication of the currency in circulation. Among these, Scottish coins predominate and silver seems to have been available up to about 1580 when billon assumes a

184 *Turner, 1614.*   **185** *Turner, 1623.*

186 Penny, 1614.

more dominant role. Some ryals and fractions come from early in the reign. Seven of these were recovered in Ayr along with almost seven hundred placks, bawbees and nonsunts. A single sword dollar of 1567 gives a probable date of deposition before 1570. This is the largest hoard known from this period and many of the others are considerably smaller.

A hoard found near Stornoway on Lewis, mainly of silver, and another, all of silver, from High Blantyre, Lanarkshire, both contained a few ryals but were mainly composed of James's debased half merks which would date concealment to the 1570s. Two quarter merks of 1572 date a further hoard, found in a cow's horn at Greenock, to about 1575. The sixty or so coins were composed mostly of some testoons as well as bawbees and nonsunts of Mary. A small weight box found on a farm near Beith in Ayrshire contained six bawbees and a one third ryal of 1567 along with twelve half merks and quarter merks of 1572-4. Probably also to be assigned fairly early in the reign is a 'very large number' of silver coins discovered near Arthur's Seat, in Edinburgh, during railway construction in 1831. It contained some groats of Henry VIII as well as Scottish issues from James V to James VI.

After 1580 silver seems to have been unavailable for hoarding or perhaps better sent to the melting pot as silver prices rose. A group of four small billon hoards is known. Twelve of the fourteen or so coins found in Niddry Street, Edinburgh, were eightpenny groats of 1583-8. Some of the 'considerable number' of coins found in a pot in Skene Road, Aberdeen, seem to have been of the same issue. A hoard of just less than one hundred coins from Noranside, Angus, was of billon issues of James V to James VI. The Edzell Castle, Forfarshire, find of twenty-eight coins was mainly of the smaller billon denominations ending with the lions or hardheads of 1588. However, billon does nor appear to have been hoarded to the same extent as in Mary's reign.

A gold hoard is also probably dated to soon after 1588 by the presence of a thistle noble. Found at Elgin, it contained a 'considerable number' of Scottish gold pieces of James V, Mary and James VI as well as a few French and Spanish coins. Several unspecified gold coins of James VI were found in Kelso in 1789 and in the same year gold coins running up to James VI were recovered from one of two hoards unearthed at Linlithgow. A few gold coins were also found, along with around four hundred balance half merks of 1592, at Bareray on North Uist.

In contrast no more than half a dozen hoards can be assigned to the first quarter of the seventeenth century. The most notable feature of these is the presence of Tudor silver as well as the post-1603 English and Scottish issues. Very few stray finds of gold or silver belong to either part of this long reign. Billon finds are more common, presumably belonging before the end of the sixteenth century, and among these the November issue of the 1588 lion or hardhead is by far the more usual type to be recovered. The 1593 plack turns up to a lesser extent as do the 1575 countermarked lions or hardheads of Mary. James VI's reign though rich in output is poor in finds of hoards and strays.

CHAPTER NINE
Charles I and the Civil War

The long reign of James VI ended with his death in late March 1625. He was succeeded by his son Charles I. Within a fortnight the King had ordered dies to be made for a new coinage. This in fact was little different from the last issue of the previous reign. There is the obvious change of royal name but, apart from a slight alteration in the form of the beard, the portrait is still that of James VI. The range of denominations is also similar and in this form Charles's first coinage lasted almost a decade.

The order for the dies was directed to the sinker, Charles Dickeson, who was also to prepare the new Scottish seals. The work had been completed satisfactorily by the summer when he received a payment of £450 for his efforts. This appears to have been additional to his yearly salary of £8 6s 8d as listed in the 'Fies of the Cunyhouse' recorded in 1620. John Achesoun, appointed in 1608, continued to hold the office of General of the Mint and George Foullis that of Master. They were to remain in their posts for the duration of the first coinage. The mint itself remained in the Cowgate.

The unit is the main gold coin with smaller numbers of the double and Britain crowns but no half-crowns or thistle crowns were struck, though they were included in the warrant from the Privy Council to the mint dated 15 April 1625. This same warrant lists the full range of silver: crown or sixty shilling piece and thirty, twelve and six shillings (**187-190**) as well as a shilling and 'halfe shilling' or sixpence. However, the last does not appear to have been struck. The types and inscriptions follow those of the last issue of James VI. The date is given only on the six shilling pieces and each year from 1625 up to 1634, except for 1629, is known. A copper twopence and penny were also ordered but did not appear.

However, a scarcity of small change resulted in the order for the latter being repeated in 1629 when 500 stone of pure copper was to be coined in twopences and pennies. These were to be of the same types as the 1623 issue with the triple-headed thistle on the obverse and the lion rampant on the reverse (**191**). Likewise the flans were to be prepared by the mill and cutter before being hammered or stamped. The

187 *First coinage, 1625-34, silver sixty shilling piece.*

188 *Similar, thirty shilling piece.*

189 *Similar, twelve shilling piece.*

190 Similar, six shilling piece, 1632.

191 Turner, 1629.

mint possessed three mills and two cutters but being 'verie meekle waisted and sindrie pairts thairof broken' the Privy Council ordered the Master of the Mint to have them repaired. Striking seems to have been completed by 1631.

In that year it was suggested that copper farthings be issued as in England so that the coinages of the two countries might correspond in copper as well as in the precious metals. The proposal was not taken up, perhaps because the twopence was too well established but officially for reasons of convenience in exchange and reckoning. A further issue of twopences was ordered at the beginning of 1632. The obverse was to have a crown over C and R with a II to indicate the value. A single-headed thistle with the legend, NEMO ME IMPUNE LACESSET was to appear on the reverse (**192**). 1,500 stone of these smaller and lighter twopences was to be struck by the end of 1634 and pennies were to be struck from time to time as the Lord Treasurer should direct, though none is known.

More importantly they were to be 'forged in a milne, cutted by cutters, printed with presses and other ingynes'. They are thus the first Scottish coins to be produced entirely by machinery. Equally important was the arrival of Nicholas Briot at the Edinburgh mint. Formerly of the Paris mint, chief graver at the Tower Mint and proponent of the use of machinery, he was sent by the King personally to produce the

192 Turner, 1630s.

turners by the new process. Also of note is the assignment of the profits of the copper coinage to the Earl of Stirling in compensation for his losses when Port Royal in Nova Scotia was surrendered to the French.

The 1,500 stone was struck over a year before the deadline and can be distinguished by the use of an English crown. The production of a similar amount commenced early in 1634. The crown, however, now takes the Scottish form. Despite a claim by the mint officials that the coins were not being properly produced, the King supported Briot who completed the task probably late in 1636. Yet a third group was ordered and started the following year. The amount was raised to 1,800 stone but all of this may not have been coined when production ceased early in 1639. By this time over 40 million had been struck and, along with the large quantities of imported forgeries, they had swamped the currency. So many possessed such turners that a great outcry followed their reduction to one penny each in November 1639. The Privy Council swiftly reversed its decision five days later. They circulated for a further three years until formally demonetized on 20 March 1642.

Meanwhile the death of the Mint Master, George Foullis, in 1635 had enabled the King to appoint Briot to the post. However, confirmation of this was delayed due to the opposition of the other mint officials and by Briot's own disinclination to agree to reside in Scotland, for fear, he said, of losing his fees from the London mint. It was not until August 1637 that the situation was resolved with the joint appointment of Briot and his Scottish son-in-law, John Falconer, to exercise all the liberties, privileges and immunities of the mastership and to 'uplift the fees and dues belonging to the said office'.

However, the monetary needs of the country could not wait while such matters were being debated. A continuing scarcity of small silver coins forced the Privy Council to order an issue of these in July 1636. Briot was directed to produce half merks, forty and twenty pence pieces but he was not permitted to use the new presses. These are the first Scottish pieces of the reign to bear the King's own portrait. Easily recognized as that of Charles I, it was prepared by Briot and then handed over to Charles Dickeson, the mint's engraver, for the production of the dies.

Both the Act of the Privy Council ordering the coinage and its warrant to Dickeson detail the types of the three proposed coins. On these, and subsequent small denominations, the title King of Scotland, England, etc. is used in place of the more normal King of Great Britain etc. The half merk has the value, six shillings and eight pence (VI/8), placed behind the head. The reverse of the latter displays the Scottish arms with the legend, CHRISTO AUSPICE REGNO ('I reign under the auspices of Christ'). The two smaller coins also bear the value, XL and XX, but possess a crowned thistle on the reverse (**193**). The legend of the forty pence reads, SALUS REIP SUPR LEX ('The safety of the state is the supreme law') while that on the twenty pence is, IUST THRONUM FIRMAT ('Justice strenghtens the throne'). Convinced of the superiority of his presses, Briot struck some pieces, with the addition of C R on the reverses, completely by machinery (**194**). These milled patterns do indeed show the superiority of milling over hammering.

193 Second coinage, 1636, Briot's hammered coinage, silver forty pence piece.

194 Similar, Briot's milled patterns, twenty pence piece.

Another problem with the currency was the disappearance of the large silver denomination and its virtual replacement by overpriced European dollars: crown-sized pieces of which the Scottish equivalent was the sixty shilling piece. At the end of 1636 it was at last resolved to call these into the mint for re-striking into twelve and six shilling pieces. Briot was agreeable to carry out the task provided that he could use the presses and, secondly, that the King would forgo the profit or seignorage. These conditions seem to have been met, for in January 1637 the Privy Council authorized Briot to produce a new coinage and ordered Dickeson to prepare the dies. The order implies a full range of silver coins and not just the two discussed the previous year.

Charles I's third coinage thus began in January 1637 and the first issue is clearly marked by Briot with his initial on all denominations. This B is to be found usually at the end of either or both legends or, less often, below the bust or above the reverse crown. Apart from this feature, the sixty shilling and thirty shilling pieces bear the equestrian portrait of the King though now facing to the left and in a more refined style than that found on the first coinage (**195**). Again on the twelve shilling, half merk, six shilling, forty and twenty pence pieces the bust, by Briot, faces left. All have the value behind the head and the larger pieces possess the letters C and R, crowned, on the reverse on either side of the coat of arms (**196-200**). The reverse of the two smaller pieces consists of a crowned thistle as on Briot's hammered coinage of 1636. The legends on all the silver remained unchanged.

Gold does not appear to have been struck until towards the end of the year. All or some of this was produced from bullion brought back from Guinea. The warrant for coining this bullion is dated 19 October and orders the coins to be of the same types as authorized in 1625 though on 14 December a change was made to the reverse legends. Striking

195 *Briot's silver issue, thirty shilling piece.*

196 Similar, twelve shilling piece.

197 Similar, half merk
(six shillings and eight pence)

198 Similar, six shilling piece.

199 Similar, forty pence piece.

200 Similar, twenty pence piece.

201 Briot's gold issue, unit.

had evidently not commenced, for only the new legends are known. That on the unit is, HIS PRAESUM UT PROSIM ('I am set over these that I may be of benefit') and is accompanied on the obverse by Briot's half length portrait of Charles (**201**). This still faces right though the new bust on the half unit, Britain crown and half-crown faces left as on the silver (**202**). The legend on these three pieces reads, UNITA TUEMUR ('We guard the union') (**203-204**). The amount is not likely to have been large and the striking of gold coins was probably over by the end of the year or soon after.

When Briot had been confirmed as Master in August 1637, he had read a letter to the Privy Council from the King saying that he should return to London as soon as possible. Briot had been active on the coinage throughout 1637 and he probably returned to England early in 1638. Whatever the precise date, sometime after there were struck a number of thirty and twelve shilling pieces similar, except for minor

202 Similar, half unit.

203 Similar, Britain crown. *204 Similar, half-crown.*

205 Intermediate issue, thirty shilling piece.

variations, to Briot's but without the initial B. These constitute the 'intermediate issue' of the third coinage (**205**). This is followed by a further two issues bearing the initial F, of John Falconer, and a final issue of the same type without his initial.

These may date from June 1639 when the newly established Committee of Estates ordered another coinage, of previous types, and appointed Captain George Foulis as General of the Mint. The

206 Falconer's first issue, twelve shilling piece.

207 Similar, forty pence piece. *208 Similar, twenty pence piece.*

Committee then entered into a contract with 'John Falconer, Master of his majesty's cunyiehous' for the issue of gold and silver coins. It would thus appear that Falconer was now sole Master and indeed there is no further mention of Briot in relation to the Scottish coinage. A small number of units and half units are known with an F in place of a B and presumably indicate a striking of gold by Falconer. The earlier of his silver issues is again similar to Briot's but for the initial and consists of twelve and six shilling pieces as well as forty and twenty pence pieces (**206-208**).

A thirty shilling piece, with an F by the horse's raised rear hoof, was included in Falconer's second issue (**209**). The lesser values of twelve and six shillings and a twenty pence piece depict the King's bust entirely within the inner circle whereas previously this broke the circle and legend to touch the outer circle (**210**). All three also bear the initial F. Another group of thirty shilling, twelve shilling and twenty pence pieces have the bust similarly treated but do not possess the initial letter (**211-212**). These are known as Falconer's 'anonymous issue' and would seem to pre-date March 1642 when a new and more restricted silver coinage was ordered. Meanwhile, in April 1641, John Alexander

209 Falconer's second issue, thirty shilling piece.

210 Similar, twelve shilling piece.

211 Anonymous issue, thirty shilling piece.

212 Similar, twelve shilling piece.

of Garthmore had replaced George Foulis as General of the Mint and he in turn was succeeded by Sir John Hope of Watterheid. The post was gifted to him by the King with a salary of £500 per annum along with all the other fees and privileges.

On 28 March 1642 the Privy Council issued a warrant for the striking of three shilling and two shilling pieces. The former has a thistle behind the head and the crowned arms on the reverse with the legend, SALUS REIP SUPREM LEX (**213**). The smaller piece bears the value, II, behind the King's head but has the old lion rampant coat of arms with the IUST THRONUM FIRMAT legend (**214**). The King's portrait is poorly executed in comparison to that on the third coinage and reflects the lesser ability of Charles Dickeson working on his own. Still employed as engraver of the dies, he is mentioned in the warrant as being responsible for these. The old dies were to be formally 'brokin and destroyed' in the presence of the the Treasurer Depute and officers of the mint. It is not known when the fourth coinage ceased but it was the last precious metal issue in Scotland for over twenty years.

213 Fourth coinage, 1642, three shilling piece.

214 Similar, two shilling piece.

215 Turner, 1640s.

At the same time a new copper coinage was ordered. The warrant for this, dated 24 February 1642, specified a return to the larger, heavier turner of which 1,500 stone was to be struck within the year. The light turners of the 1630s were to be current only until 20 March. The new pieces have the letters C and R crowned on the obverse and a thistle on the reverse with the NEMO ME IMPUNE LACESSET legend (**215**). A Further 1,500 stone was ordered in November 1644. These may have taken longer to strike for the warrant was extended until November 1646. Another 1,000 stone was struck in 1648 and a small amount in 1650. In all, it has been estimated, that over 11 million of these turners were struck thoughout the period 1642-50. They are distinguishable by the use of a single initial mark, a lozenge, on each side. No further coins were struck in Scotland until after the Restoration.

Given the large number of turners struck by Charles I, it is not surprising that they are among the most common of seventeenth-century site finds. Despite their poor weight and appearance those of the 1630s were hoarded, thus confirming the impression often given by the records that they were the only coins readily available to the populace at large. Among a half dozen hoards, that from Knowehead, Banffshire, contained about 2,000 pieces while a little hoard hidden in the thatched roof of Toward Castle, Argyllshire, before 1642 came crashing down and scattered over the the floor of the hall when Toward was burnt by the Campbells in 1646. The hoard of 128 found at Pow, Stromness, Orkney, in 1955 provided the material for the current arrangement of this coinage.

Gold seems to have been scarce during Charles I's reign in Scotland and no single find seems to have been recorded. It is known to have been included in only two published hoards. Two English gold coins were found among a large, but poorly recorded, find from Strathblane, Stirlingshire, and ten – one Scottish and nine English of James VI and I – are included in the 1,375 coins discovered outside Kelso in 1991 and probably hidden in 1643. Not surprisingly there is a marked rise in the number of hoards which have survived from the civil war years up to the execution of the King in 1649. These usually consist of silver but with only small numbers of Scottish coins, mainly the smaller denominations – forty and twenty pence pieces. The majority are English ranging from worn and clipped Elizabethan shillings and sixpences struck between 1561 and 1603 to sixpences and shillings of James I and shillings and half-crowns of Charles I. The largest denomination, as consistently noted in the government records, consists of the foreign 'dollar', especially of the Spanish and United Netherlands but also a whole range of German and Austrian issues. Charles I's Scottish currency was truly European.

CHAPTER TEN
Restoration to Union 1660-1707

There was a hiatus of over a decade in the Scottish coinage coinciding with the Commonwealth. Charles I was already dead when the small issue of turners took place in 1650 but these properly belong to his copper coinage of the 1640s. Although Charles II had been crowned at Scone at the beginning of 1651, he was in no position to consider a new coinage until after the restoration in 1660. However, coinage matters then moved quickly. A new General, Charles Maitland, was appointed before the year was out and in January 1661 the privileges of the mint officials were confirmed.

Two Acts of Parliament passed on 12 June 1661 ordered copper and silver coinages respectively. After lying idle for so long the mint and its machinery needed refurbishment and it was not until 1663 that the Master, still Sir John Falconer, reported that all was ready and requested a warrant to commence striking the turners. It would appear that no design had been ordained for Falconer further asked to be allowed to strike pieces similar to those of the last coinage of the 1640s but with the addition of II to indicate they belonged to Charles II. His petition was granted.

Production began at the end of July and these turners can be easily recognized by the small II placed after the crowned CR in the centre of the obverse (216). Parliament had decreed that 3,000 stone should be struck and this seems to have been completed by 1666. Yet the mint continued to issue turners at an increasing rate without the

216 Charles II, turner, 1663.

government realizing what was happening. By the time minting ceased in July 1668 a further 5,000 stone had been struck, giving an estimated total of over 23 million turners. The dies were then destroyed before the Privy Council. These turners from the years 1663-8 possess a great variety of initial marks, among which a cross is most common.

Meanwhile the silver coinage had also appeared. The Act of 1661 specified the coining of pieces of four merks, two merks, one merk, a half merk and forty pence. However, about eighteen months elapsed before the King signed a warrant addressed to Thomas Simon to produce puncheons for these as well as a range of four gold coins. There is no evidence that the latter were ever made and no gold coins are known from this reign. Simon was paid £100 for over 150 puncheons, and this work was among the last major commissions given to one of the Royal Mint's most famous engravers, who died in 1665. The puncheons were received by Maitland, the General of the Edinburgh Mint in 1663 and he in turn passed them on to Joachim Harder for the manufacture of the dies. In October 1663 the Privy Council ordered the two merk, merk and half merk pieces but did not include the four merk piece until March 1664. However, no coin seems to have been issued with the date 1663 and all four run from 1664. The forty pence piece was not struck.

All four denominations bear Simon's bust of Charles II, laureate and facing right. The legend is quite simple, CAROLUS II DEI GRATIA, and, as ordered by the Privy Council, there is also 'a litle thistle or secreit mark' (**217-220**). This thistle was at first placed above the head but was soon moved to beneath it, where it remained for most of this

***217** Four merks, 1664.*

218 Two merks, 1664.

219 Merk, 1664.

220 Half merk, 1673.

coinage. Only towards the end was it replaced by the letter F. This stands for the younger Sir John Falconer since his father, Master of the Mint from 1637, had died in 1671. It would appear that son succeeded father at that time.

The reverses of the silver coins contain the four coats of arms set in a cruciform pattern with those of Scotland first and third and those of England second and Ireland fourth. In the centre is the mark of value in shillings and pence, LIII/4, XXVI/8, XIII/4 and VI/8 respectively. Between the arms is a crowned pair of interlinked Cs. The legend gives the King's title, MAG BRI FRA ET HIB REX, and ends with the date. The mint registers show that all or some of the four values were struck each year from 1664 until 1675. There appears to have been a concentration on the two larger pieces in the early years and again in 1670 when over 20,000 of each were coined. Small numbers of merks and half merks were produced from 1664 to 1668 and then large numbers of merks each year until 1675, except for 1674. About 400,000 merks were struck in 1671 alone but in only one year did the number of half merks exceed 20,000. This first coinage seems to have come to an end in June 1675.

In the course of 1674 the chief engravers at the Royal Mint, the three Roettiers brothers, had been ordered by Charles to prepare new puncheons, matrices and dies for another Scottish coinage. Again it seems a gold coinage was intended and again it never materialized. In April 1675 the Roettiers signed a receipt for £150 sterling payment for this work. Meanwhile the mint buildings had been thoroughly repaired and new presses and other machinery were then purchased from the London mint. At the beginning of the year the King had instructed the Privy Council to make changes to the reverse designs of the silver coins and to strike five denominations of these types from the four merk to forty pence piece. The five coins of the second coinage are now referred to as the dollar, half, quarter, eighth and sixteenth dollar (221-225).

221 Dollar, 1682.

222 Half dollar, 1675.

223 Quarter dollar, 1676.

224 Eighth dollar, 1676.   225 Sixteenth dollar, 1677.

The portrait was also changed though no reference to this is to be found in any of the known records. It is more simple and tidy, without the mass of hair found on Simon's portrait, and now faces left. The changes to the reverses are of a minor nature. The coats of arms are given a crown above and changed to those of Scotland, England, France and Ireland. A thistle is placed between these, while the value, now discarded, is replaced by a single pair of interlinked Cs. Also the

King is described as of 'Scotland and England' rather than of 'Great Britain' but otherwise the legends are similar and the date is retained. The new forty pence piece, however, possesses as its reverse a saltire with a crown over the centre and the national emblems of a thistle, rose, lis and harp in the angles. In 1681 the values of the coins were raised to fifty-six, twenty-eight, fourteen and seven shillings and the forty pence to forty-two pence.

The mint register suggests the second coinage commenced in November 1675. Although this ends in December 1681, some pieces with the date 1682 are known but this is the latest date to occur. A small number of half, quarter and eighth dollars are dated 1675. The dollar is first dated 1676 and up to 1682 approximately 20,000 were struck. Small numbers only of the half dollar were issued in 1675, 1676 and 1681. The quarter dollar and eighth dollar are the most common and were struck each year of the coinage. Well over half a million quarter dollars and 120,000 eighth dollars were produced. The sixteenth dollar appeared in much smaller numbers, and only for 1677 and 1681 with the former being much more numerous.

Despite the huge numbers of turners issued in the 1660s, it would seem that copper had become scarce by the second half of the 1670s and that much French copper was in circulation. In 1677 therefore the Privy Council ordered a new coinage in this metal to the amount of 3,000 stone to be struck within three years. It was to consist of a bawbee of sixpence (**226**), last struck in billon in Mary's reign, and a turner (**227**). Although called a turner in the official records the term 'bodle' was now being frequently applied to the twopenny piece. Bawbees are found with the dates 1677, 78 and 79 and though the turners or bodles bear the same dates, only 1677 is common. Again, as in the 1660s, the mint appears to have greatly exceeded the authorized numbers. This at least had the effect of ending the shortage of copper coin.

226 *Charles II, bawbee, 1677.*   **227** *Similar, bodle, 1678.*

The bawbee bears a portrait similar to that found on the silver coinage though the King's name and titles are given on the obverse. The reverse consists of a crowned thistle with the NEMO ME IMPUNE LACESSET legend ending with the date. The obverse type of the turner is a crown over a crossed sword and sceptre while the reverse is also a thistle. The legends are similar to those on the bawbee but the date appears over the thistle rather than the crown. The sheer number of these, however, must have come to the attention of the government and aroused suspicion.

The King indeed set up a Commission in 1682, 'Appoynted for tryall of the Minte of Scotland'. The officers seem to to have co-operated fully, with the exception of the General, Charles Maitland Lord Haltoun. Brother of the once mighty Secretary for Scotland, the Duke of Lauderdale, he probably saw the danger to himself as Lauderdale slipped from power towards death that year. However, even if set up for political reasons, the Commission had no difficulty in uncovering a string of abuses. In its report, presented on 4 August 1682, the Commissioners listed charges not only of greatly exceeding the amount of copper coins authorized but also others including low weight, poor fineness, lack of assays of the silver coinage and the drawing of salaries, in some cases twice over, for non-existent work. The Commission reported that it estimated at least £699,873 Scots had been embezzled.

The mint was closed down. At the end of August the King wrote to the Lord Chancellor and Privy Council removing Lord Haltoun, Sir John Falconer, Alexander Maitland the Warden and Archibald Falconer from their positions and ordering their prosecution for corruption. In 1683 they were found guilty to the sum of £72,000 sterling. Charles Maitland, now Earl of Lauderdale following his brother's death, was fined £20,000 and Sir John Falconer the equivalent of four and a half years' rent on his estates though this was later commuted to £3,000. In the end he was forced to sell his estates to pay this. The mint's equipment seems to have been removed by the government with the felicitous result that nearly 200 years later a group of 109 punches, matrices and dies was presented to the Society of Antiquaries of Scotland. Now preserved in the National Museums of Scotland, these implements, belonging to the silver coinage of 1675-82 and the copper coinage of 1677-9, are a remarkable reminder of seventeenth-century minting and misdemeanour.

The mint was still closed when Charles II died in 1685 and was succeeded by his brother, James VII and II. Sir John Falconer seems to have harboured a hope that the new King would restore him to office but it was not to be and he died early in 1686. Parliament clearly did not want to see a repetition of the events of the previous reign. It passed a detailed act 'on matters relating to the Mint' in June 1686. A free coinage was proposed, proper Trials of the Pyx were to be carried out and the weight of the silver coinage was reduced so that it now stood at 13:1 instead of 12:1 in relation to sterling. A coinage of five silver denominations was proposed, along with gold and copper if thought necessary. New salaries were fixed for the officers giving the new General, Richard, Lord Maitland, £3,600 Scots and the Master, Sir William Sharpe, £2,400.

228 *Forty shilling piece, 1688.*

229 *Ten shilling piece, 1687.*

No gold or copper was in fact struck for James VII. Of the five silver pieces, the sixty, forty, twenty, ten and five shillings, only the forty and ten shilling pieces were issued (**228-229**). Both bear a bust of James to the right in the style of the Roettiers - presumably the engravers once more. The titles are given on the reverse and, as MAG BRIT is used, James is designated the 'Second' instead of the 'Seventh'. The reverse of the forty shilling piece consists of the crowned arms and for the first time the edge of the coin is lettered, with the inscription NEMO ME IMPUNE LACESSET and the regnal year. Coins dated 1687 occur with both ANNO REGNI TERTIO and QUARTO and 1688 with QUARTO. The ten shillings bears a crossed pair of sceptres with the four national emblems between. Its edge is merely grained. The values, 40 and 10 respectively, are to be found under the King's bust.

The events of 1688 and 1689 brought about the replacement of James VII by William and Mary. Forty and ten shilling pieces with the date 1689 suggest dies were produced that year though it would appear that they were not used until later since the mint remained closed. New mint officials were being chosen with Lord Cardross taking over as General and William Denholme as Master. The previous officials were slow to move out of the lodgings and the Privy Council, in January 1690, ordered them 'immediately to flitt and remove themselves their wyfes bairns and families'. The King and Queen signed a warrant, at Kensington Palace early in February, for the issue of the full range of five silver coins, although it was only on 26 September that it was brought before the Privy Council. The same day a proclamation was issued for the re-opening of the mint.

230 Sixty shilling piece, 1691.   *231 Forty shilling piece, 1691.*

In this reign all five silver denominations were issued with the conjoined busts of William and Mary facing to the left (**230-234**). The values appear under the bust, though on the five shilling piece the roman V is used, at first on the reverse before being moved to under the busts. The crowned coat of arms, now with an extra shield bearing the lion of Orange, is the reverse type on the four large denominations. However, on the five shilling piece it consists of a crowned W & M monogram. Only the forty shilling piece is found with each date from 1689 to 1694 and the year of the reign, PRIMO to SEXTO, on the edge. The edge inscription was changed to, PROTEGIT ET ORNAT ('It protects

232 Twenty shilling piece, 1693.   *233 Ten shilling piece, 1691.*

234 Five shilling piece, 1694.

and adorns') which also occurs on the sixty shillings though this was struck only in 1691 and 1692. Again only two dates, 1693 and 1694, are found on the twenty shillings. The ten shillings bears all dates except 1693 while the five shillings was issued only in 1691 and 1694.

No gold was struck for William and Mary but a copper coinage of turners or bodles and bawbees was issued. This had been ordered by an Act of Parliament passed on 19 July 1690 which authorized the production of 3,000 stone weight to be completed within six years with one-third being sixpences and the remainder twopences. The bawbee bears the royal portraits with their names and titles and, on the reverse, the usual thistle and NEMO legend ending with the dates 1691-4 (**235**). The obverse of the bodle consists of a somewhat neater W & M monogram and titles while the reverse type copies that on the bawbee (**236**). Striking began on 1 October 1691 but was cut short by the death of Mary at the end of December 1694.

Within the week, on 2 January 1695, the Privy Council ordered that the dies bearing the late Queen's portrait and name were to be used no longer. On 11 July it issued a warrant for the striking of forty and ten shilling pieces. Apart from the change to the bust of William alone and

235 Bawbee, 1692. *236 Bodle, 1692.*

237 Forty shilling piece, 1696.

a corresponding alteration in the royal name and titles, these are similar to those of the joint reign. The forty shillings possesses the same inscription on the edge as before but with the regnal years seventh to twelfth (**237**). All dates from 1695 to 1700 exist though the last is scarce. Twenty shilling and ten shilling pieces were struck each year from 1695 to 1699 (**238-239**). It is not clear if a sixty shilling piece was ever struck for William alone. A piece dated 1699 is said to have existed but, if it is extant, its present whereabouts is unknown. On the five shilling pieces, dated 1695 to 1702 except for 1698, the W & M monogram is replaced by a crowned thistle (**240**).

The order to cease using the dies with the conjoined portraits had included those for the copper coins. However, the six year contract for these was nearing its time limit and the Master of the Mint accordingly petitioned the Privy Council for permission to proceed with making blanks while new dies were being prepared. This was granted. In July the Privy Council decided on the necessary changes in type and ordered the mint's engraver, John Clerk, to cut the dies.

238 Twenty shilling piece, 1695.   **239** Ten shilling piece, 1697.

240 Five shilling piece, 1699.

On the bawbee (**241**) the King's head was to appear alone while on the bodle the monogram was to be replaced by a crossed sword and sceptre with a crown above. Bodles of 1695 have the sword and sceptre flat at first (**242**) but they then become more erect (**243**). Bawbees and bodles exist only for 1695-7 when it is thought the contract for the 3,000 stone of copper was completed. Parliament, in October 1699, allowed for a further 3,000 stone but no action was taken on this.

241 Bawbee, 1695.

242 Bodle, with low sceptres, 1695.   *243 Similar, with high sceptres.*

In addition to the silver and copper, a small coinage in gold was also struck in William's name. This was the first such striking in the noble metal since the reign of Charles I and also the last gold of the Scottish coinage. The initiative came from the Directors of the Company of Scotland Trading to Africa and the Indies. Better known for its disastrous Darien expedition, the Company did do some trading to Africa and there obtained a quantity of gold dust. The Directors sought to have this turned into coin 'for the honour and interest of the kingdom' and to have some reference on the coins to the Company. The Privy Council agreed in 1700 to the issue of gold twelve and six pound pieces with the Company's crest of a rising sun below the King's bust. The reverse bears the royal arms and the legends the royal name and titles. Dated 1701 they are commonly known as pistoles and half pistoles (244-245).

244 Gold pistole, 1701.   *245 Gold half pistole, 1701.*

The King died in March of the following year to be succeeded by his sister-in-law Anne, the younger daughter of James VII. Queen Anne's Scottish coinage, however, was to be somewhat modest. Indeed it was not until January 1705 that the Privy Council issued a warrant to James Clerk to engrave the dies and then only for ten and five shilling pieces. By March these were ready when the mint was ordered to re-open and

246 Ten shilling piece, 1705.

247 Five shilling piece, 1705.

to proceed with coining. The two denominations exist with the dates 1705 and 1706 though the five shilling piece seems to have been struck in much the greater numbers (**246-247**). The Queen's portrait faces left and is accompanied, on the larger piece, by a coat of arms, now without the lion of Orange. The thistle continues as the reverse type on the five shillings but later in 1705 the royal titles replaced the NEMO legend. The title of Great Britain was soon to indicate a political union instead of merely a union of the two crowns thus making the issues of 1706 the last of a separate Scottish coinage.

The first post-Union British coins of 1707 were to be of the same types, standards and values as those then current in England. The denominations were to be the crown, half-crown, shilling and sixpence with those to be struck in Edinburgh to have the addition of an E under the Queen's head (**248-252**). There had been a major re-coinage of older money in England in 1696 and the same was now necessary for Scotland. One of the chief officials then responsible was the Warden, Isaac Newton, and now Master of the Royal Mint since 1699, Sir Isaac Newton oversaw the operation in Edinburgh. Workmen, machinery and puncheons for the dies were sent north to assist the Scottish mint and ensure similar working practices. By mid-1709 the work of converting the Scots coins, along with foreign silver and some older English

248 Crown, 1707, with E below bust for Edinburgh.

249 Half-crown, 1708.

250 Shilling, 1707.

251 Sixpence, 1708.

252 Crown, 1708, struck at the Tower Mint, London.

milled silver, was complete. All four new denominations were struck with the dates 1707 and 1708 but only the half-crown and shilling with 1709.

Despite the commitment of Article XVI of the Act of Union to the continuation of a mint in Edinburgh, these were the last coins to be struck in Scotland. It is surprising, perhaps, that there was no outcry among the mint officials either against the virtual take-over by Sir Isaac Newton or the cessation of production. It may be that such an outcome had been understood or expected and, in any event, the posts and more importantly their attached salaries remained intact. In fact they continued until 1817. Sixty years later the defunct mint buildings were demolished. However, more than enough coins have survived to bear witness to one of Europe's most interesting and vibrant coinages.

Select Bibliography

Armet, H. 'Sir John Falconer of Balmakellie, Master of the Scottish Mint', *The Scottish Genealogist* 14 (1967), 1-9

Bateson, J. D. and Mayhew, N. J. *Sylloge of Coins of the British Isles: 35 Scottish Coins in the Ashmolean Museum, Oxford and the Hunterian Museum, Glasgow* (Oxford, 1987)

Bateson, J.D. 'Roman and medieval coins found in Scotland, to 1987', *Proceedings Society Antiquaries Scotland* 119 (1989), 165-88

Bateson, J.D. *Scottish Coins* (Shire Album 189, Princes Risborough, 1987)

Bateson, J.D. *Coin Finds from Cromarty* (Cromarty Courthouse, 1993)

Burns, E. *The Coinage of Scotland* (Edinburgh, 1887)

Brown, I.D. and Dolley, M. *A Bibliography of Coin Hoards of Great Britain and Ireland 1500-1967* (London, 1971)

Cochran-Patrick, R. W. *Records of the Coinage of Scotland* (Edinburgh 1876)

Crawford, B. E. *Scandinavian Scotland* (Leicester, 1987)

Curle, J. *A Roman Frontier Post and its People: the Fort of Newstead* (Glasgow, 1911)

Dolley, R. H. M. *Sylloge of Coins of the British Isles: 8 The Hiberno-Norse Coins in the British Museum* (London, 1966)

Editorial Note, 'The 1969 Colchester Hoard', *British Numismatic Journal* 44 (1974), 39-40

Graham-Campbell, J.A. 'The Viking-Age silver and gold hoards of Scandinavian character from Scotland', *Proceedings Society Antiquaries Scotland*, 107 (1976), 114-135

Holmes, N. M. McQ. *Weill Wrocht and Cunyeit, The Edinburgh mint and its Coinage* (Edinburgh, 1982)

Holmes, N.M. McQ. 'A fifteenth-century coin hoard from Leith', *British Numismatic Journal* 53 (1983), 78-107

Hocking, W. J. 'Notes on a collection of coining implements in the National Museum of Antiquities, Edinburgh', *Proceedings Society Antiquaries Scotland* 49 (1915), 308-31

Keppie, L. *Scotland's Roman Remains* (2nd ed., Edinburgh, 1990)

Mayhew, N.J. 'The Aberdeen, St Nicholas Street hoards of 1983 and 1984', *British Numismatic Journal* 58 (1988), 40-68

Metcalf, D. M. (ed.), *Coinage in Medieval Scotland (1100-1600)* (BAR 45, Oxford, 1977)

Murray, J. E. L. 'The early unicorns and heavy groats of James III and James IV', *British Numismatic Journal* 40 (1971), 62-96

Murray, J. E. L. 'The first gold coinage of Mary Queen of Scots', *British Numismatic Journal* 49 (1979), 82-6

Murray, J. E. L. 'The coinage of the Marians in Edinburgh Castle', *British Numismatic Journal* 57 (1987), 47-53

Murray, J. E. L. and J. K. R. 'Notes on the vicit leo testoons of Mary Queen of Scots', *British Numismatic Journal* 50 (1981), 81-90

Murray, J. K. R. 'The Stirling bawbees of Mary Queen of Scots', *Numismatic Circular* 74 (1966), 94

Murray, J. K. R. 'The Scottish coinage of 1553', *British Numismatic Journal* 37 (1968), 98-109

Murray, J. K. R. 'The Scottish silver coinage of Charles II', *British Numismatic Journal* 38 (1969), 113-25

Murray, J. K. R. 'The Scottish gold and silver coinages of Charles I', *British Numismatic Journal* 39 (1970), 111-44

Murray, J. K. R. 'The billon coinages of James VI of Scotland', *Numismatic Chronicle* 132 (1972), 177-82

Murray, J. K. R. 'The Scottish gold coinage of 1555-8', *Numismatic Chronicle* 139 (1979) 155-64

Murray, J. K. R. and Stewart, I. 'The Scottish copper coinages 1642-97', *British Numismatic Journal* 41 (1972), 105-35

Reece, R. *Coinage In Roman Britain* (London, 1987)

Ritchie, A. *Viking Scotland* (London, 1993)

Robertson, A. S. 'The circulation of Roman coins in North Britain: the evidence of hoards and site-finds from Scotland' in *Scripta Nummaria Romana: essays presented to Humphrey Sutherland*, eds. R A G Carson and C M Kraay (London, 1978) 186-216

Robertson, A. S. 'Roman coins found in Scotland, 1971-82', *Proceedings Society Antiquaries Scotland* 113 (1983), 405-48

Robertson, A. S. *The Antonine Wall* (4th ed., Glasgow, 1990)

Seaby, P. and Purvey, P. F. *Coins of Scotland, Ireland and the Islands* (Seaby Standard Catalogue of British Coins, vol. 2, London, 1982)

Sekulla, M. F. 'The Roman coins from Traprain Law', *Proceedings Society Antiquaries Scotland* 112 (1982), 285-94

Smart, V. *The Coins of St Andrews* (St Andrews University, 1991)

Stevenson, R. B. K. 'The "Stirling" turners of Charles I, 1632-9', *British Numismatic Journal* 29 (1959), 128-51

Stevenson, R. B. K. *Sylloge of Coins of the British Isles: 6 National Museum of Antiquities of Scotland, Edinburgh: Part I Anglo-Saxon Coins* (London, 1966)

Stevenson, R. B. K. 'The Anglo-Saxon penny and its context' 339-41 in Morris, C. D. and Emery, N. 'The chapel and enclosure on the Brough of Deerness, Orkney: survey and excavations, 1975-1977', *Proceedings Society Antiquaries Scotland* 116 (1986), 301-74

Stevenson, R. B. K. 'The bawbee issues of James V and Mary', *British Numismatic Journal* 59 (1989), 120-56

Stevenson, R. B. K. 'The groat coinage of James V, 1526-38', *British Numismatic Journal* 61 (1991), 37-56

Stevenson, R. B. K. and Porteous, J. 'Two Scottish seventeenth-century coin hoards', *British Numismatic Journal* 41 (1973), 136-46

Stewart, I. *The Scottish Coinage* (2nd ed., London, 1967)

Stewart, I. 'Scottish Mints' in *Mints, Dies and Currency*, ed. R A G Carson (London, 1971) 165-289

Stewart, I. 'The long voided cross sterlings of Alexander III illustrated by Burns', *British Numismatic Journal* 39 (1970), 67-77

Stewart, I. 'The Scottish element in the 1969 Colchester hoard', *British Numismatic Journal* 44 (1974), 48-61

Stewart, I. 'Two Centuries of Scottish Numismatics' in *The Scottish Antiquarian Tradition*, ed. A S Bell (Edinburgh, 1981) 27-65

Stewart, I. and North, J. J. 'Classification of the single-cross sterlings of Alexander III', *British Numismatic Journal* 60 (1990), 37-64

List of Illustrations

1 Antoninus Pius for Marcus Aurelius, dupondius or as, AD 153-4, found in the changing-room of the bath-house at Bearsden.
2 Vespasian, denarius, AD 69-70, found in the aedes at Old Kilpatrick.
3 Trajan, denarius, AD 103-11, found in the annexe at Balmuildy.
4 Julius Caesar, denarius, 49-48 BC, found at Elginhaugh.
5 Brutus and Cassius, denarius, 43-42 BC, found at Elginhaugh.
6 Plated hybrid denarius of Vespasian and Vitellius, AD 73, found at Elginhaugh.
7 Mark Antony, legionary denarius (Leg. V), 32-31 BC, found at Bearsden.
8 Vespasian, Fides as, struck at Lyons (with globe at end of neck), AD 77-8, found outside the officers' quarters end of barrack block 5 at Elginhaugh
9 Domitian, unworn Moneta as, AD 86, found near the west gate adjacent to the commandant's house at Elginhaugh.
10 Domitian, unworn Moneta as, AD 85, found in the destruction level of the officers' quarters of barrack block 5 at Elginhaugh.
11 Antoninus Pius, sestertius, AD 143, with Victory and BRITAN on reverse.
12 Antoninus Pius, as, AD 154-5, with Britannia on the reverse.
13 Tin copy of denarius of Trajan, AD 112-17, from the well at Bar Hill.
14 Similar.
15 Similar.
16 Similar.
17 The latest certain coin find from a site on the Antonine Wall: Marcus Aurelius for Lucilla, denarius, AD 164-9, found at Old Kilpatrick.
18 Commodus, sestertius, AD 184-5, with title BRIT at end of obverse legend and VICT BRIT in exergue on reverse.
19 Septimius Severus, denarius, AD 201-10, with title BRIT at end of obverse legend and Victory with the legend VICTORIAE BRIT on the reverse.
20 Septimius Severus for Caracalla, dupondius, AD 206-10, reverse depicting Victory with the legend VICTORIAE BRITANNICAE.
21 Julius Caesar, denarius, 49-48 BC, found at Leckie Broch.
22 Trajan, denarius, AD 101-2, found at Leckie Broch.
23 Eanred (810-41), styca, moneyer Eadwin.
24 Eanred, styca, moneyer Fordred.
25 Aethelred II, first reign (841-4), styca, moneyer Tidwulf.
26 Aethelred II, second reign (844-9), styca, moneyer Eardwulf.
Nos. 23-6 are probably from the Glenluce Sands, Wigtownshire.
27 Aethelred II, first reign, styca, moneyer Eanred, found 1988 on the sandhills at Baleshare, North Uist. [enlarged x 2]
28 Machrie hoard (Islay), Eadgar (959-75), penny, moneyer Durand.
29 Machrie hoard, Eadgar, penny (fragmentary), moneyer ?Wiferth.
30 Machrie hoard, Eadgar, penny (fragmentary), uncertain moneyer.

LIST OF ILLUSTRATIONS

31 Iona hoard, Eadred (946-55), penny, moneyer Thurmod.
32 Iona hoard, Eadwig (955-9), penny, moneyer Heriger.
33 Iona hoard, Eadgar (959-75), penny, moneyer Grid.
34 Iona hoard, Eadgar, penny, moneyer Fastolf.
35 Quendale hoard (Shetland), Eadwig (955-9), penny, moneyer Aescwulf.
36 Quendale hoard, Eadgar (959-75), penny, moneyer Heriger.
37 Quendale hoard, Aethelred II (978-1016), penny, crux type (991-7), York, moneyer Wulfsige.
38 Piece of ring-money from the Skaill hoard (reproduction in the Hunterian Museum, Glasgow University).
39 Aethelred II, penny, crux type (991-7), Cambridge, moneyer Edric, found at the Brough of Birsay, Orkney, 1979.
40 David I, period C, penny, Roxburgh, Hugo, about 1150.
41 William I, crescent and pellet penny, with pommée sceptre head, Edinburgh, Adam, 1186-95.
42 William I, short cross penny, phase A, 1195-1205, Edinburgh, Hue, [HVE: ONEDNEBVR].
43 William I, short cross penny, phase B, 1205-30, struck by the moneyers Hue and Walter working together [hVE-WALTER].
44 Alexander III, long cross penny, class II, Glasgow, Walter, [WA/LT/ER'O/NG].
45 Alexander III, long cross penny, class III, Edinburgh, Alexander, [AL/EXO/NED/EN].
46 Alexander III, long cross penny, class VII, Glasgow, Walter,[WA/LT/ERON/GLA].
47 Alexander III, second coinage, 1280-86, penny, with neat hair, and four mullets of six points giving twenty-four points on the reverse.
48 Alexander III, second coinage, halfpenny.
49 Alexander III, second coinage, farthing.
50 Alexander III, second coinage, penny, with swept hair, and two mullets of six points and two stars of seven points giving twenty-six points.
51 John Baliol (1292-6), rough issue, penny.
52 John Baliol, smooth issue, penny.
53 Robert I, penny, about 1320.
54 Robert I, halfpenny.
55 Robert I, farthing.
56 David II, penny, 1350-57.
57 David II, heavy groat, with D in one angle of the reverse.
58 David II, heavy coinage, 1357-67, halfgroat, group A, Aberdeen.
59 David II, heavy coinage, groat, group A, Edinburgh.
60 Similar, group B, Aberdeen.
61 Similar, group C, Edinburgh.
62 Similar, group D, Edinburgh.
63 David II, light coinage, 1367-71, groat, Edinburgh.
64 Similar, penny.
65 Robert II (1371-90), groat, Edinburgh.
66 Similar, halfgroat.
67 Similar, penny.
68 Similar, halfpenny.
69 Robert III, heavy coinage, 1390-1403, groat, with pellets on cusps, Edinburgh.
70 Similar, with trefoils on cusps.
71 Robert III, heavy halfpenny, Perth.
72 Robert III, light coinage, 1403-06, groat, Edinburgh.
73 James I, fleur-de-lis groat, first variety, 1424, Edinburgh.

LIST OF ILLUSTRATIONS

74 Similar, second variety.
75 James II, fleur-de-lis groat, third variety, 1437-51.
76 James II, crown and pellets groat, 1451-60, Edinburgh.
77 Similar, Aberdeen.
78 Similar, Stirling.
79 James III, mullet groat (group I), 1467, Edinburgh.
80 Similar, Berwick.
81 James III, light mullet groat (group IV), Edinburgh.
82 James III, first portrait groat (group II), 1471-83, Edinburgh.
83 James III, second portrait groat (group VI), 1484-8, Edinburgh.
84 James IV, heavy groat, 1489-96, without numeral.
85 James IV, light groat, 1496-1513, without numeral.
86 Similar, with QRA.
87 Similar, with IIII.
88 Similar, with medieval 4.
89 James V, second coinage, 1526-38, groat, type I.
90 Similar, type II.
91 Similar, type III.
92 Similar, one third groat, type IV.
93 David II, noble, 1357.
94 Robert III, heavy lion, 1390-1403.
95 Robert III, heavy demi-lion.
96 Robert III, light lion, 1403-06.
97 James I, demy, 1424-37, with large quatrefoils with open centres.
98 James II, lion, 1451-60.
99 James III, rider, 1475-83, with rider to right.
100 Similar, rider to left.
101 Similar, half rider.
102 James IV (1488-1513), unicorn, second type, with crown of five lis on unicorn.
103 James IV, half unicorn.
104 James V, first coinage, 1513-26, gold unicorn.
105 James V, second coinage, 1526-38, gold crown.
106 James V, third coinage, 1538-42, gold ducat, 1539.
107 Ducat, 1540.
108 Two-thirds ducat, 1540.
109 One-third ducat, 1540.
110 James III, billon plack.
111 Similar, half plack.
112 James III, copper farthing, type I, with crown on obverse. [enlarged x2]
113 Similar, type II, with IR crowned on obverse and a crown over a saltire cross on the reverse. [enlarged x2]
114 Similar, type IV, with large trefoil on obverse and a cross with crowns and mullets on the reverse. [enlarged x2]
115 James III, copper crux pellit penny, type I.
116 Similar, type II.
117 Similar, type III.
118 James IV, billon plack.
119 James IV, billon penny, second issue, with round bust (IV).
120 James V, first coinage, 1513-26, billon plack.
121 James V, third coinage, 1538-42, billon bawbee.
122 Similar, half bawbee.
123 Similar, bawbee with annulets. Mary – regency (1542-58)
124 Billon bawbee, 1542-58, Edinburgh.
125 Similar, with fluted cross.
126 Similar, half bawbee.
127 Bawbee, Stirling, 1544.
128 Gold crown, 1543.
129 Gold twenty shilling piece, 1543.
130 Billon penny, with infant head, 1547.
131 Gold forty-four shilling piece, 1553.
132 Similar, twenty-two shilling piece.
133 Silver portrait testoon (group I), 1553.

LIST OF ILLUSTRATIONS

134 Gold three pound piece, 1555.
135 Similar, thirty shilling piece.
136 Testoon (group II), 1555.
137 Testoon (group III), 1558.
138 Billon lion or hardhead, 1555.
139 Billon 'vicit veritas' penny, 1556.
140 Billon 'servio' plack, 1557.
Francis and Mary (1558-60)
141 Silver testoon, 1559.
142 'Vicit leo' testoon, 1560.
143 Similar, half testoon.
144 Billon nonsunt, 1559.
145 Billon lion or hardhead, 1559.
Mary – personal rule (1561-7)
146 Mary, first widowhood, portrait testoon, 1561.
147 Similar, half testoon.
148 Mary and Henry, silver ryal, 1565.
149 Similar, two-thirds ryal.
150 Similar, one-third ryal.
151 Mary, second widowhood, ryal, 1567.
152 Similar, one-third ryal.
James VI (1567-1603)
153 Silver ryal or 'sword dollar', 1570.
154 Similar, two-thirds ryal, 1569.
155 Silver half merk or noble, 1573.
156 Similar, quarter merk 1572.
157 Countermarking of 1575 – heart and star, on Mary 'servio' plack, 1557.
158 Gold twenty pound piece, 1575.
159 Countermarking of 1578 – crowned thistle, on Francis and Mary testoon, 1558.
160 Silver two merk or thistle dollar, 1579.
161 Gold ducat, 1580.
162 Silver thirty shilling piece, 1582.
163 Gold lion noble, 1585.
164 Similar, two-thirds lion noble.
165 Billon eightpenny plack, 1583-90.
166 Similar, half plack.

167 Hardhead or twopenny plack, August 1588.
168 Similar, November 1588.
169 Similar, half hardhead or penny.
170 Gold thistle noble, 1588.
171 Gold hat piece, 1592.
172 Silver balance half merk, 1592.
173 Billon saltire plack, 1594.
174 Gold rider, 1594.
175 Silver ten shilling piece, 1593.
176 Silver five shilling piece, 1595.
177 Copper turner or twopence, 1597.
178 Gold sword and sceptre piece, 1602.
179 Half sword and sceptre piece, 1601.
180 Silver thistle merk, 1602.
James VI and I (1603-25).
181 Silver sixty shilling piece, 1604-09.
182 Gold double crown, 1609-25.
183 Silver twelve shilling piece, 1609-25.
184 Turner, 1614.
185 Turner, 1623.
186 Penny, 1614.
Charles I (1625-49)
187 First coinage, 1625-34, silver sixty shilling piece.
188 Similar, thirty shilling piece.
189 Similar, twelve shilling piece.
190 Similar, six shilling piece, 1632.
191 Turner, 1629.
192 Turner, 1630s.
193 Second coinage, 1636, Briot's hammered coinage, silver forty pence piece.
194 Similar, Briot's milled patterns, twenty pence piece.
Third coinage 1637-42
195 Briot's silver issue, thirty shilling piece.
196 Similar, twelve shilling piece.
197 Similar, half merk (six shillings and eight pence),

198 Similar, six shilling piece.
199 Similar, forty pence piece.
200 Similar, twenty pence piece.
201 Briot's gold issue, unit.
202 Similar, half unit.
203 Similar, Britain crown.
204 Similar, half-crown.
205 Intermediate issue, thirty shilling piece.
206 Falconer's first issue, twelve shilling piece.
207 Similar, forty pence piece.
208 Similar, twenty pence piece.
209 Falconer's second issue, thirty shilling piece.
210 Similar, twelve shilling piece.
211 Anonymous issue, thirty shilling piece.
212 Similar, twelve shilling piece.
213 Fourth coinage, 1642, three shilling piece.
214 Similar, two shilling piece.
215 Turner, 1640s.
216 Charles II, turner, 1663.
Charles II first silver coinage 1664-75
217 Four merks, 1664.
218 Two merks, 1664.
219 Merk, 1664.
220 Half merk, 1673.
Second silver coinage 1675-82
221 Dollar, 1682.
222 Half dollar, 1675.
223 Quarter dollar, 1676.
224 Eighth dollar, 1676.
225 Sixteenth dollar, 1677.

226 Charles II, bawbee, 1677.
227 Similar, bodle, 1678.
James VII (1685-9).
228 Forty shilling piece, 1688.
229 Ten shilling piece, 1687.
William and Mary (1689-94)
230 Sixty shilling piece, 1691.
231 Forty shilling piece, 1691.
232 Twenty shilling piece, 1693.
233 Ten shilling piece, 1691.
234 Five shilling piece, 1694.
235 Bawbee, 1692.
236 Bodle, 1692.
William II (1694-1702)
237 Forty shilling piece, 1696.
238 Twenty shilling piece, 1695.
239 Ten shilling piece, 1697.
240 Five shilling piece, 1699.
241 Bawbee, 1695.
242 Bodle, with low sceptres, 1695.
243 Similar, with high sceptres.
244 Gold pistole, 1701.
245 Gold half pistole, 1701.
Anne (1702-14)
Before Union
246 Ten shilling piece, 1705.
247 Five shilling piece, 1705.
Post Union
248 Crown, 1707, with E below bust for Edinburgh.
249 Half-crown, 1708.
250 Shilling, 1707.
251 Sixpence, 1708.
252 Crown, 1708, struck at the Tower Mint, London.

Scottish Monarchs from 1100-1707

Alexander I	(1107-1124)
David I	(1124-1153)
Malcolm IV	(1153-1165)
William I	(1165-1214)
Alexander II	(1214-1249)
Alexander III	(1249-1286)
Margaret	(1286-1290)
John	(1292-1296)
Robert I	(1306-1329)
David II	(1329-1371)
Robert II	(1371-1390)
Robert III	(1390-1406)
James I	(1406-1437)
James II	(1437-1460)
James III	(1460-1488)
James IV	(1488-1513)
James V	(1513-1542)
Mary	(1542-1567)
James VI	(1567-1625)
Charles I	(1625-1649)
Charles II	(1649-1685)
James VII	(1685-1689)
William and Mary	(1689-1694)
William II	(1694-1702)
Anne	(1702-1714)

Index

A

Abbasid coins 30
Abbey crown 83-4, 99
Aberdeen, finds from 41, 47, 53
Aberdeen, hoards from 52-3, 68, 111, 127
Aberdeen mint 40, 46, 60, 64, 67, 75, 86, 87, 88
Aberdour hoard 58
Achesoun, James 70, 83, 84-5, 95
Achesoun, John 102, 105, 107, 108, 129
Achesoun, Thomas 116
Aedes 13
Æthelred II, King of England 32, 35, 58
Æthelred II, King of Northumbria 27, 28, 30
Aethelstan, King of England 30, 35, 38
Aethelwulf, King of Wessex 30
Agricola, Governor of Roman Britain 11
Albany, John Duke of 82
Alexander II 43, 47
Alexander III 43, 45, 48, 50
Alfred the Great, King of Wessex 35
Angus, Archibald Earl of 83
Anne, Queen 155-6
Antonine Wall 18-21
Antoninus Pius, Emperor 12, 20, 21, 22
Arcadius, Emperor 25
Arran, James Earl of 82-3, 97, 99, 100-01

As, the 9
Auchendavy Roman fort 19
Augustus, Emperor 22
Aureus 9
Ayr, finds from 47, 53, 86, 87, 88
Ayr, hoards from 68, 127
Ayr mint 45

B

Badinsgill hoard 43
Balance half merk 120
Balmuildy Roman fort 13
Balgoney Farm, Perthshire, hoard 60-61, 76
Bamborough Castle mint 40
Bannockburn, Battle of 50
Bar Hill Roman fort 19, 21
Barr Hoard 95
Bawbee 95-6, 97-8, 148-9, 152-4
Bearsden Roman fort 12, 19, 20, 26
Beith hoard 127
Beonna, King of East Anglia 35
Berwick 51, 65, 66, 80
Berwick Castle 41
Berwick, find from 44
Berwick mint 40, 41, 43, 46, 49-51, 65, 80
Billon 86-96
Birrens Roman fort 19, 21, 22, 26
Black money 91-4
Bodle 152, 154
Bonagio of Florence 58
Bonnet piece 84
Bothwell, Earl of 110
Briglands hoard 23
Briot, Nicholas 131-8

169

INDEX

Britain crown 124
Britannia 19, 23
Britannia as 19, 25
Brodgar hoard 35, 37
Broomholm hoard 16
Brough of Birsay 38
Brough of Deerness 37
Brussels hoard 46
Burgred, King of Mercia 30, 37
Burgundian gold coins 81, 85
Burray hoard 32, 37
Bute hoard 40, 41

C

Cadder Castle hoard 78
Caldale, Kirkwall, hoard 35, 37, 38
Cambuskenneth Abbey, finds from 43, 47, 61
Camelon Roman fort 22
Caracalla, Emperor 24
Cardean Roman fort 13, 15, 17
Cardross, Lord 151
Carlisle mint 39-40
Carpow Roman fortress 24
Carriden Roman fort 14, 19
Carsphain hoard 52
Carstairs hoard 21
Cassius Dio 23
Castledykes Roman fort 14, 22, 26
Charles I 93, 129-42
Charles II 143-9
Clerk, James 155
Clifton hoard 70
Clipping 45
Cochrane 92-3
Cockburnspath hoard 30, 38
Coenwulf, King of Mercia 30
Coinless hoards 35
Cokin, John 47
Colchester hoard (1969) 46
Cologne, denier of 31, 38
Commodus, Emperor 15, 21, 23
Constantine the Great, Emperor 26
Copper coins 86, 90-94, 122

Corbridge mint 39
Corehead, gold mined at 85
Corry, John 58
Countermark, cinquefoil 82-3
Countermark, crowned thistle 114
Countermark, heart and star 113
Cowie Moss hoard 24
Cnut, King of England 35, 38
Cramond Roman fort 23-4, 26
Cranston, Thomas de 64
Crawford Roman fort 13, 17
Crawford Muir, gold mined on 85
Creggan hoard 94-5
Crescent and pellet penny 41
Crieff Church hoard 76
Crispina, Empress 15
Cromarty, finds from 44, 47
Crossraguel Abbey hoard 93
Crown, Scottish 124
Crown and pellets groat 64, 78, 87
Croy hoard 30, 38
Crux pellit penny 91, 93
Cut coins 43, 45, 47

D

Dalginross Roman fort 15
Dalkeith, mint moved to 113
Darien Expedition 155
Darnley, Henry Lord 108-09
Dates, introduction of on coins 84
David I 39
David II 54-9, 71, 73, 74-5
Debasement 72-3, 86
Demi Lion 75
Denarius 9
Denholm, William 151
Denier 27, 30, 31, 38
Depreciation 72-3
Derling, Raul 41
Devaluation 73
Dickeson, Charles 129, 133, 134
Dirham 27, 30, 31, 35, 38
Diocletian, Emperor 25
Dollars, European 134, 142

INDEX

Domitian, Emperor 11, 15, 17, 22
Double tournois 122
Dryburgh Abbey hoard 78
Ducat 84
Dull hoard 35, 37, 38
Dumbarton mint 60, 75
Dumfries hoard 81
Dumfries mint 46, 47
Dunblane hoard 85
Dundee mint 58, 116
Dunrossness hoard 35, 38
Dunscore hoard 68
Duntocher Roman fort 19
Dun Hiadin hoard 43
Dun Lagaidh hoard 43
Duns Castle hoard 52
Dupondius 9
Dyke hoard 41

E

Eadgar, King of England 31, 32, 35, 37, 38
Eadmund, King of England 37
Eadred, King of England 37
Eagle crown 82, 95
Eanbald, Archbishop of York 27
Eanred, King of Northumbria 27
Easter Happrew Roman fort 17
Écu à la couronne 75
Eddleston hoard 70, 85
Edinburgh Castle 41, 101, 102, 113
Edinburgh, hoards from 60-61, 68, 127
Edinburgh mint 28, 41, 42, 46-7, 49, 51, 54-6, 58, 59-60, 62, 63, 65, 66, 67, 70, 75, 80, 86, 87, 88, 89, 90, 94, 98-99, 100, 102, 116, 124, 129, 143, 149, 156-8
Edwardian pennies 50, 52-3, 59
Edward III, King of England 51, 54, 58-9, 68, 71, 74, 75, 76, 78, 85
Edward IV, King of England 65, 68
Edward Baliol 52-3
Edward the Elder, King of Wessex 30

Edzell hoard 127
Elgin hoard 128
Elginhaugh Roman fort 15-17
Elizabeth I, Queen of England 112, 124
Erebald 39

F

Falaise, Treaty of 41
Falconer, Archibald 149
Falconer, Sir John 132, 138, 143, 145
Falconer, Sir John, the Younger 145, 149
Falkirk hoard 24-5
Farthing 48
Faustina I, Empress 13
Fendoch Roman fort 15
Flemish gold coins 75, 77
Fleur-de-lis groat 62-3, 87
Flodden Field, Battle of 82
Forfar mint 46
Forgeries 60, 110-111, 113, 117
Forres, David 102
Fortrose hoard 60
Fort Augustus hoard 25
Foulis, Captain George 137
Foulis, Thomas 116
Foullis, George 125, 132
Francis, Dauphin and King of France 97, 105-08
Frankish deniers 31, 38
French gold coins 75, 77, 81, 82, 85, 111, 128
French subsidy 77

G

Galba, Emperor 15
Galston 35
General of the Mint, post of 102
Geta, Emperor 23-4
Glasgow, finds from 44
Glasgow, hoards from 111

Glasgow mint 43, 46, 47
Glasgow Cathedral hoard 75-6
Glenluce hoards 47, 68, 88, 94
Glen Afton hoard 68
Gold, native 83, 85
Greenock hoard 127
Gray, Robert 63, 77-8
Groat 54-73
Guinea, gold from 134, 155

H

Hadrian, Emperor 16, 20
Hadrian's Wall 18
Hakate, Robert 63
Halfgroat 54
Halfpenny 48
Haltoun, Lord - see Maitland, Charles
Harald Hardrada, King of Norway 35, 38
Hat piece 119-120
Hawick hoard 111
Hazelrigg hoard 47
Henri II, King of France 105
Henry I, King of England 39
Henry II, King of England 41-2
Henry III, King of England 45
Henry VI, King of England 61, 81
Henry VII, King of England 70
Henry VIII, King of England 70, 85, 99, 111, 127
Henry, Prince 39-40
Hertford, Earl of 99
Hiberno-Norse pennies 34-5, 37, 38
High Blantyre hoard 127
Hilton Farm, Perthshire, hoard 78
Hochstetter, Joachim 70
Holyrood, mint at 83-4, 102, 116
Holywood Church, finds from 44
Honorius, Emperor 25
Hope, Sir John 140
Hopetoun papers 99, 101
Hue Walter, joint moneyers 42, 43
Hugo 40

I

Iona, Abbot's House hoard 32
Inchaffrey Abbey, finds from 47, 53
Inchkenneth hoard 32-4, 38
Inchtuthil Roman fortress 15
Innerwick hoard 80-81, 93
Inveresk Roman fort 14
Inverness mint 46, 47

J

James I 61-2, 77-8, 80-81, 85, 87
James II 62, 64, 77-8, 80-81, 87-8
James III 65-7, 72, 78-80, 81, 86, 88-93
James IV 68-9, 70, 80-81, 94-5
James V 69-70, 72, 82-5, 86, 95
James VI and I 113-28
James VII and II 150-151
Jedburgh, finds from 35, 38, 41, 42, 44
Jedburgh hoard 70
John Baliol 50

K

Keith hoard 43
Kelso hoards 128, 141-2
Kennedy, Bishop, of St. Andrews 93
Ker, John 63
Killichonate Farm, Inverness-shire, hoard 61
Kilmarnock hoard 68
Kinghorn mint 46, 47
Kirk o' Banks hoard 35, 37
Kinneil Roman fortlet 19
Knowehead hoard 141
Knox, John 108

L

Lanark, finds from 44
Lanark mint 46, 47
Lauderdale, Duke of 149

INDEX

Lauderdale, 3rd Earl of - see Maitland, Charles
Lauder Bridge 92
Leckie Broch, finds from 25, 61
Legionary pay, Roman army 11
Leith hoard 88
Leuchars hoard 24
Lindores hoard 35, 38
Lingrow Broch, finds from 25
Linlithgow hoards 70, 128
Linlithgow mint 62-3, 78
Linlithgow Palace 63
Lion 75
Lion noble 117
Lion rampant, introduction of on coins 74
Livingstoun, Alexander 65, 79
Lochar Moss hoard 78
Lollius Urbicus, Governor of Roman Britain 18
Long cross penny 45-7
Lucilla, Empress 21
Luss hoard 81
Lyons, Roman mint at 17

M

Macdonalds of the Isles 87
Machinery, use of in the mint 122, 129-131, 143, 146, 149
Machrie hoard 30-31, 38
Maeatae 23
Maitland, Charles, 3rd Earl of Lauderdale 143-4, 149
Maitland, Richard 150
Malcolm IV 40
Marcus Aurelius, Emperor 21-2
Mark 9
Mark Antony, legionary denarius of 16, 22
Marrakesh, gold dinar of 38
Mary of Guelders 78
Mary of Guise 97, 99,101-03, 106
Mary Queen of Scots 69-77
Mary Tudor, Queen of England 105

Matilda, the 'Empress' 39
Mauchline hoard 70
Maundy, the Royal 69
Megray hoard 24
Meinard 40
Melrose, the Chronicle of 42
Merk 9
Mints, physical location of 63
Misserwie, James 102
Modern losses of Roman coins 26
Moneta as of Domitian 17-18, 25
Moneta Pauperum 90-91
Montrave hoard 52, 58
Montrose mint 46, 47
Mulekyn, Donatus 54, 58
Mulekyn, James 58
Mumrills Roman fort 19-21

N

Napier, Sir Archibald 116
Newark, Deerness, Orkney 37
Newcastleton hoard 47
Newstead Roman fort 11, 15-17, 19-21, 23, 26
Newton, Sir Isaac 156, 158
Noble 74-5
Nonsunt 106-07
Noranside hoard 127
Northumbria, the Kingdom of 9, 27
North Uist hoard 32
Nudry, Robert 63, 94

O

Offa, King of Mercia 9
Olav Kyrre, King of Norway 37, 38
Old English lettering 80
Old Kilpatrick Roman fort 13, 19-21
Orkney 37-8
Orkney, Earldom of 37
Orrok, Alexander 84, 95-6
Otho, Emperor 22
Overstrike 60

P

Paisley hoard 27
Paris mint 101, 108, 131
Parton hoard 52
Penny 9, 27, 30
Perth, finds from 41, 44, 47, 53, 86, 93
Perth hoards 68, 81, 85
Perth mint 40, 41, 42, 43, 46, 47, 58, 59, 60, 62, 78, 86, 88, 116
Philip II, King of Spain 105
Pirlie pig 95
Pistole 155
Plack 68, 89, 93-5, 104
Plotina, Empress 22
Portmoak hoard 24
Port Glasgow hoard 31
Portrait groats 65-7
Portuguese gold coins 84, 110
Pound, sterling 9
Pow hoard 141
Privy marks 54, 62, 64, 88, 96, 104, 144-5

Q

Quadrans 9, 22
Quendale hoard 34

R

Raul 42
Renfrew hoard 52
Renfrew mint 46, 47
Renaissance, the 67
Restoration, the 141, 143
Revaluation 73, 114, 148
Rhoneston hoard 47, 88-9
Richard II, King of England 77
Rider 79-80, 121
Rigghead hoard 111
Ring-money 31, 32, 34, 35, 36, 37
Robert the Bruce 50-1
Robert II 56-9

Robert III 59-61, 71, 73, 75-6, 78, 86
Robert, Duke of Albany 59, 61
Roettiers, the 146-8, 150
Roman lettering 80, 82, 95
Roman Republic, coins of 15-16, 22, 24-5
Ross, Bishop of, mission to France 98
Roxburgh Castle 41
Roxburgh mint 40-43, 46, 64, 88
Roxburgh, siege of 64
Rumbling Bridge hoard - see Briglands hoard
Rus, Henri le 42
Rutherglen hoard 47
Ryal 108-09

S

Saevar Howe 37, 38
Samanid coins 30
St. Andrew, depiction of 75, 80
St. Andrews, Bishop of, right to coin 50
St. Andrews hoards 68, 81
St. Andrews mint 40, 46, 49
Scotichronicon, the 42
Scone, coronation at 61
Sculptor's Cave 25
Seignorage 58, 70, 123-4
Septimius Severus, Emperor 11, 23-4
Seton's, Lord, painter 116
Severus Alexander, Emperor 24
Sharpe, Sir William 150
Shetland 37
Shilling 9
Short cross penny 42-5, 47
Silver 27
Simon, Thomas 144
Sixty shilling piece 125
Skaill hoard 30, 37, 38
Spanish gold coins 85, 128

INDEX

Stephen, King of England 39, 42
Stevenston sands, Ardeer 35, 38
Stewart, Archibald 116
Stirling mint 46, 62-4, 78, 87, 98-9
'Stirling' turners 93, 131-2
Stornoway hoard 127
Stracathro Roman fort 15
Strageath Roman fort 17
Stranraer hoard 21, 22, 26
Strathblane hoard 141
Styca 9, 27-30
Sword and sceptre piece 122-3

T

Talnotrie hoard 27, 30, 38
Tara, Battle of 32
Tarbet hoard 31, 37
Tealby penny 41-2
Testoon 101
Thistle crown 124-5
Thistle, first depiction of on coin 66
Thistle dollar 114
Thistle noble 119
Tiree hoard 31
Titus, Emperor 15
Tod, Alexander 78, 88
Tod, Thomas 65, 79
Tom A' Bhuraich hoard 43
Tor, Adam 58
Toward Castle hoard 141
Tower Hill, London, Royal Mint on 124
Trajan, Emperor 19, 20, 22
Tranent hoard 59
Traprain Law 25
Treasure Trove, early case of 81-2
Trial of the Pyx 63, 78, 83, 150
Trotternish, Skye, hoard 30, 38
Tudor, Margaret 80
Tudor silver coins 128, 142
Turner 122, 125, 129-132, 141, 143-4, 152

Turnour, William 81-2
Twenty pound gold piece 114

U

Udal, The 35, 38, 45
Unicorn 79-80
Union, the Act of 9, 156, 158
Union of the Crowns 124
Unit 124
'Usual money of Scotland' 71-2

V

Valerian, Emperor 25
Vespasian, Emperor 13, 15, 19, 22
Vicus 14
Virius Lupus, Governor of Roman Britain 23, 24
Votadini 25

W

Walter 47
Wardlaw, Richard 84, 96
Whitburn hoard 68, 81
Whithorn Priory, finds from 27, 35, 38
Wick hoard 81
Wigmund, Archbishop of York 28, 30
Wilam 47
Wilderness Plantation Roman fortlet 19
William the Lion 40-44
William and Mary 151-2
William II and III 153-5

Y

York, fall of, to Vikings 27
York, Hiberno-Norse kings of 37
York, Vikings at 30
Young, Richard 84, 96